The Good News According to JESUS

DONALD BLOSSER PH.D

Copyright © 2024 **Donald Blosser Publishing**

All rights reserved. No part of this publication may be reproduced, distributed, or transmitted in any form or by any means, including photocopying, recording, or other electronic or mechanical methods, without the prior written permission of the publisher, except in the case of brief quotations embodied in critical reviews and certain other noncommercial uses permitted by copyright law. For permission requests, write to the publisher, addressed "Attention: Book Rights and Permission," at the address below.

Published in the United States of America

ISBN 978-1-962730-32-7 (SC)
ISBN 978-1-963379-55-6 (HC)
ISBN 978-1-962730-34-1 (Ebook)

Donald Blosser Publishing
1725 Juniper PL Apt 303
Goshen Indiana 46526
donwb@goshen.edu

Order Information and Rights Permission:

Quantity sales. Special discounts might be available on quantity purchases by corporations, associations, and others. For details, contact the publisher at the address above.

For Book Rights Adaptation and other Rights Permission. Call us at toll-free 1-888-945-8513 or send us an email at admin@stellarliterary.com

The Good News According to Jesus

The Message & Resurrection of Jesus for the Mission of the Church

I. Introduction 1

II. The Good News of Jesus 6

   1. Matthew 3:13-15   Baptism by John 6
   2. Mark 1:14-15   Mark's Introduction 6
   3. John 3:16-17   John's Statement 7
   4. Mark 1:16-20   Jesus and the Disciples 9
   5. Luke 4:16-21   Jesus at Nazareth 11
   6. Matthew 5-6-7   The Sermon on the Mount 13
   7. Matthew 11:2-16   Jesus answers John 15
   8. Matthew 25:31-46   At the Judgment Seat 17
   9. Luke 19:1-10   New Life for Zacchaeus 20
  10. Mark 11:11, 15-19   The "Cleansing" of the Temple 22
  11. Matthew 28:18-20   The Great Commission 26
  12. Acts 13:28-31   Diversity in Telling the Story 29

III. Did Jesus Have to Die? 33

IV. The Resurrection Life 39

   1. Introduction 39
   2. Resurrection in the Ministry of Jesus 40
   3. The Resurrection Story for Paul 42
   4. The Resurrection Body 43
   5. Resurrection in the Biblical Narrative 49
   6. What Does the Resurrection Story Tell Us? 50
   7. Resurrection For All Humanity 52
   8. Resurrection as Witness to Salvation 53

V. The Resurrection as Mission in God's New Age 56

VI. An Apocryphal Resurrection Narrative 63

VII. Bibliography 64

The Good News According to Jesus
I. Introduction

The Bible says. . . . was a very common phrase heard in my childhood. It carried a lot of power, because what the Bible says controlled what we believed, how we behaved, and where we went to find ultimate truth. The Bible was God's word, revealing those things that God wants us to know. We did not discuss what the Bible says, we simply read it, and obeyed it.

In I Corinthians 13:11 Paul writes: *"when I was a child, I spoke like a child, I thought like a child, I reasoned like a child; when I became an adult, I put an end to childish ways."* Today, even though we are adults, we have a strong tendency to continue reading the Bible in childlike ways.

As I became an adult, my deep appreciation for the Bible grew even stronger. It was not by accident that I dedicated my adult life to the study and teaching of the Bible. As an adult I learned that the Bible was not given to us directly from God, but was written by specific human beings who were not aware that they were writing scripture that would be studied, exegeted, and argued over for thousands of years. I learned that it is important to know who the specific New Testament writer was, what his (they were all male) experience was with Jesus, and what was the original culture in which this person lived. It was also exciting to explore, as carefully as possible, why they wrote and what the message was that they wanted their immediate readers to know. We now accept God's inspiring presence in these writers but they were not aware of this divine presence with them as they wrote.

It took longer for me to recognize that, as the Biblical writers wrote, God did not give them knowledge that was superior to, or different from, the common knowledge of their day. Moses, Joshua, Isaiah, or Paul, each assumed the earth was flat, because that was the common wisdom of the day.

The same would be true for genetics, good medical health care, or demon possession as an explanation for bizarre human social behaviors.

As followers of Jesus who read the Bible as Scripture, we assume that we are reading as mature adults, carefully discerning the Jesus message of salvation through his death on the cross. That is what I was taught as a child, and I accepted it as the only Biblical explanation for the mission and death of Jesus. I was taught that the Bible has one unified message, thus no matter where you read, it is the same story. But as an adult, I began to see things that led me to reread the gospels looking for how Jesus explained his mission, and what he said his followers should do in response. I discovered that even in the four gospels, the writers tell the same story differently, and they do not all have exactly the same explanation for how best to understand the crucifixion of Jesus.

As I prepared for my "Jesus and the Gospels" class at Goshen College I found seven different metaphors or theological images being used. And each image had a Bible verse to support it.

For example:

I Cor. 15:3	*Christ died for our sins in accordance with the scriptures...* (penal redemption)
I Peter 2:21	*Christ suffered for you, leaving you an example that you should follow in his steps* (Moral Influence)
Romans 5:10	*if...while we were enemies, we were reconciled to God by the death of his son, how much more shall we be saved by his life?* (Recapitulation)
Col. 2:15	*He disarmed the principalities and powers and made public example of them—triumphing over them by the cross* (Christus Victor)
I Peter 1:18	*You were ransomed from the futile ways inherited from your ancestors...with the precious blood of Christ.* (Ransom)
I Peter 2:24	*he himself bore our sins in his body on the cross...by his wounds you have been healed* (Substitionary Atonement)
Mark 1:14-15	*Jesus came preaching the good news of God, saying: The time has come, the kingdom of God is at hand, repent and believe this good news* (Messianic)

How does one decide which theory is the correct one, or is most biblical if even the biblical writers provide conflicting explanations? Each one, except the Mark 1 Messianic theory, has another person (Peter or Paul) interpreting the mission and death of Jesus. Mark cites words from Jesus to explain his own mission. Should that statement be seen as being closer to how Jesus saw the content of his ministry? But even there, it is Mark who decided to use this statement by Jesus to explain his ministry.

The biblical writers did not have an official, agreed-upon-by-everyone explanation for the death of Jesus. Throughout its history, the church has struggled with this question. How does one determine the exact meaning that should be used to understand this critical question of Christian Faith? Why did Jesus die on the cross?

Dr. Matthew Black was my mentor in graduate school. He insisted that when studying the Bible, we must ask two questions: 1. What does the Bible say? and 2: Why did the writer say it? It is imperative that we understand the experience and the intention of the Biblical writer if we are to correctly read and interpret the scriptures. Each writer had a message and a mission that led them to write. Luke & Matthew each had a specific audience in mind and it was not the same cultural or religious audience, thus they do not always say exactly the same thing. Paul was not just writing general theological principles, he had a specific congregation in mind as he offered his best counsel with the confidence that he had the mind of God as he wrote. (I Cor. 7:40b)

I also learned that the Anabaptists felt it was important to pay special attention to the teachings of Jesus as he lived in Palestine during that first century. I began to see a difference between believing doctrinal facts about Jesus, and being a follower of the teachings of Jesus. How did Jesus explain his own ministry? What instructions did he give his followers?

Jesus began his ministry in response to the preaching of John the Baptist (Matt.3:13-17). He explained his mission in a visit to his hometown synagogue in Nazareth (Lk 4:16-30). Matthew later summarized the basic themes in the Jesus message in what we now call the Sermon on the Mount (Matt 5-6-7). It is stated again in how Jesus answered John when John was confused about what Jesus was doing (Matt 11:2-6); and then again near the end of his ministry (Matt. 25:31-46). Jesus gave an active expression to this message in a public demonstration in the temple (Jn 2:13-16, cf Mark 11:11,15-19). Matthew's gospel closes with instructions by Jesus to his disciples about this mission (Matt. 28:18-20).

These texts should not be treated as verbatim quotes of what Jesus said, but rather as the basic content that the early Christian community remembered and focused on as they met together in worship. It is legitimate to believe these statements give a reasonably appropriate report of things Jesus said and did during his ministry. If Jesus came strictly for the purpose of dying for our sins, there is no reason for him to teach, heal, or challenge people to live by God's New Way. All he had to do to be faithful to his God-determined mission was die, nothing else mattered. And if that was actually why he came, one would expect that his concern for the disciples would be that they get their theology right, and know for sure that his death was spiritually intentional and purposeful. That would mean that Judas, the Jewish Sanhedrin, and Pilate were all doing exactly what God intended for them to do. His death would have been "Mission Accomplished".

It would be helpful if we could gather together as followers of Jesus and do what Mark, Peter and Paul did, share together how the life and death of Jesus has changed our lives, and not demand that every one of us must have the same experience, or accept the same theological explanation. We could then move on together as followers of Jesus, extending the ministry begun by Jesus in a world that sorely needs to see Jesus come alive in our midst.

The teaching mission of Jesus focused on the presence of God's New Way, where his own life was the living example of what this New Way would be like. His death shows how truly radical God's New Way of living is. It also demonstrates what a threat God's New Way was to the Sanhedrin and the powers of Rome.

By killing Jesus Rome felt they had solved a potential political problem, and the Sanhedrin believed they had avoided significant disruption in the religious life of the nation. They had restored the peaceful way things were before John the Baptist, then Jesus, began challenging their authority.

The process for this study is (as much as possible) to allow the text to speak for itself. As a graduate of Anabaptist Mennonite Biblical Seminary, I learned the Inductive Bible Study method under Dr. Howard Charles, the finest New Testament teacher I ever had. This process was continued in graduate school at St. Andrews University in Scotland where I was privileged to study with Dr. Matthew Black who also insisted that a Biblical scholar goes to the text, not to find evidence that proves what you already believe, but to go deeper into what the text itself says.

I begin this study by reading again the four New Testament gospels, searching for what Jesus said about himself and his mission. Then we look at Paul, how he understood Jesus, and how he shaped the developing life of the New Testament Church. Third, we will look at the resurrection of Jesus, and how this shaped the church, and how the church shaped this resurrection message.

It is not my goal for this study to find the absolute final and unquestionable truth. Rather, I invite the reader to walk with me in exploring the Biblical message of how Jesus spoke about his mission. Then integrate what the early church did with that message, finding new life after that dreadful crucifixion experience by rallying together around the teachings of Jesus and the message of the resurrection.

It is a challenge to step outside what one has always believed and explore the biblical message as if for the first time. It is likely that much of what we find will affirm what we already believe, but we do not start there. We begin by trusting the text to speak for itself.

II. The Good News of Jesus

1. Matthew 3:13-15   Baptism by John

Then Jesus came from Galilee to John at the Jordan, to be baptized by him. But John would have prevented him, saying, "I need to be baptized by you, and do you come to me?" But Jesus answered him, "let it be so now; for it is proper for us to fulfill all righteousness." Then he consented.

Matthew opens the public ministry of Jesus with an extended treatment of family stories surrounding the birth of Jesus. Then he connects the ministry of Jesus with the preaching of John the Baptist.

John had a message of repentance, saying that God's New Age is coming. He called Israel to prepare for this new age which he saw as a new restoration of Torah for Israel (Matt. 3:2-3). The common people heard this as a message of hope and they flocked to John for baptism in preparation for the coming of God's new age. Jesus also went to John for baptism. The Biblical writers saw the baptism of Jesus as commissioning for his own message which was a continuation of the John message of Torah repentance. But Jesus made one important change in John's message content. John the Baptist proclaimed that the new age was coming, while Jesus said this new age is already here as a present reality (Mark. 1:14-15).

2. Mark 1:14-15   Mark's Introduction of the Jesus Message

Now after John was arrested, Jesus came into Galilee, proclaiming the good news of God, and saying, "The time is fulfilled, and the kingdom of God has come near; repent and believe in the good news."

After John was arrested by Herod, Jesus began his ministry. He came to Galilee with a message from God, saying: **The kingdom of God has come near, repent and believe the good news**". For Mark the content of the good news was directly connected with the presence of God's New Way. Mark was writing after the crucifixion. He connects the good news with the message Jesus was preaching rather than with the death of Jesus on the cross.

The other gospel writers reflect similar content. Though not identical, each one is similar in content. Matthew links Jesus with the Torah renewal message of John the Baptist. Luke cites the return of Jesus to Nazareth in celebration of the Year of Jubilee (Lk 4:16-30). John has Jesus calling disciples (Jn.1:29-51) implying that Jesus is planning for a long term mission of teaching God's New Way, and he is starting the process by training a symbolic group of twelve to keep the message alive. In each of the gospels, the message of Jesus is connected to this new understanding of Torah that is to be lived out in God's New Way.

3. John 3:16-17   John's Statement of the gospel

"For God so loved the world that He gave his only Son, so that everyone who believes in him may not perish but have everlasting life. Indeed, God did not send the Son into the world to condemn the world, but in order that the world might be saved through him."

The focus of the ministry of Jesus is contained in one of the most well known statements made by Jesus in his conversation with Nicodemus. But because of our assumptions about the death of Jesus we read things into the text that are not there. The text begins: *"For God so loved the world that He gave. ."* and we assume that everyone knows this means God gave Jesus to die for our sins.

Having made that assumption, we quickly accept two theological concepts: this shows the tremendous love of God in that God was willing to sacrifice God's own Son so that we might be saved. The second is that only Jesus could pay this price because he was sinless. But this raises alternative questions. Does God really demand the death of one person as the price of forgiveness for other persons? This presents an unacceptable view of the nature of God. It does not reflect how Jesus talked with the disciples about God.

Is this an accurate reading of what the text says, or are we inserting our own beliefs into the text in a way that significantly changes what Jesus is saying? It is perfectly valid to say that God loved the world so much that God gave. But God's gift to humanity was sending Jesus to live among us and share God's vision for a New Way. In this message God's mercy is not dependent on having someone die before God will show mercy. It puts a new focus on the life and teaching ministry of Jesus, which is far more consistent with the image of God that Jesus gives. But since this is not the traditional reading that we are most comfortable with we immediately challenge any other reading of the text even when the traditional reading creates serious theological problems.

This reading of John 3:16 is consistent with Jesus in the Garden of Gethsemane on the last night of his life. Jesus went there with the disciples, leaving them to "watch and pray" while he went further into the garden for his own quiet time with God. Three times he prayed the same prayer *"let this cup pass from me, yet not what I want, but what you want." (Matt. 26:29, 40,44)*.

Matthew has Jesus pouring out his heart to God, asking "isn't there some other way to do this?" This leads to the question: if dying for the sins of humanity was the original, defining purpose for the ministry of Jesus, would Jesus here be asking God to change the mission? But if God sent Jesus to share a message of new life that reflects God's original and primary intention for all humanity, then it would be quite logical for Jesus to ask "is my death the only way to do this? This is not the message you gave me to share with humanity."

If one holds a more traditional view of God that says God knows all things, then it could be that God knew if Jesus lived a life that was faithful to the intentions of God, the possibility of death was quite real. Thus Jesus lived with the awareness that faithful living carries the threat of death. The gospels report several times that the religious authorities thought about trying to kill Jesus. But this does not mean that God sent Jesus with the explicit intention of dying. It simply accepts the reality that faithful living might lead the forces of evil to attempt to silence the messenger by killing him or her. Unfortunately, the reality of death is still a present danger for those who dare to live the radical truth of God's New Way.

Moving ahead to the next day, Jesus has been tried and sentenced to death. He is now on the cross and his humanness bursts forth in a dramatic cry, "*My God, My God, why have you forsaken me?* (Matt. 26:46). If Jesus came with the explicit mission to die in order to save sinners, this cry makes no sense because by his death, horrible and painful as it was, he was fulfilling God's perfect plan for human redemption.

But if Jesus is saying "I can understand the disciples running away, I can even understand Peter denying that he ever knew me, but dear God, why have YOU forsaken me, leaving me here to die alone." This statement puts new meaning into the death of Jesus. It was not God's eternal plan for Jesus to die, but the firm commitment of Jesus to remain faithful in his relationship with God meant that Jesus had to face death rather than defy or deny that relationship. God did not sacrifice Jesus. That is not how God does things. Jesus sacrificed himself. The content of his God message challenges us to accept death at the hands of our enemies rather than kill our enemies to save ourselves. In the death of Jesus we truly see the immeasurable depth of God's love.

4. Mark 1:16-20   Jesus and the Disciples

As Jesus passed along the Sea of Galilee, he saw Simon and his brother Andrew casting a net into the sea, for they were fishermen. And Jesus said to them, "Follow me and I will make you fish for people." And immediately they left their nets and followed him. As he went a little farther, he saw James son of Zebedee and his brother John who were in their boat mending their nets. Immediately he called them; and they left their father Zebedee in the boat with the hired men, and followed him.

When Isaiah (8:16) and Jeremiah, (26:7-8) both formed small schools, they were making a statement about the content of their message. They expected their message would live on long after the teaching prophet was no longer alive.

When Jesus intentionally called a group of men to be with him, he was making a statement about his own message much like these Old Testament prophets. The number twelve has an obvious connection with the twelve tribes of Israel, leading to the belief that Jesus was initiating a new Israel based on a new understanding of Torah. He also expected this message would have long term implications for the people of Israel.

This is an important statement about how Jesus saw his own ministry. If he came with the primary purpose of dying for the sins of humanity, there would be no need for disciples. His death would have completed God's salvation activity. Thus, there would be nothing salvific in the deaths of any of the disciples even though several of them did die as martyrs. In traditional theology their deaths had no salvific merit for others because they themselves were sinners and they could only die for their own sins.

Therefore, the simple act of Jesus calling disciples says that Jesus had a long range perspective that went far beyond his own personal ministry. He was thinking in terms of a renewal movement based on a fresh reading of Torah living. The disciples were to give leadership to this long term ministry that went far beyond Jesus himself.

This concern for the long range future of his teaching ministry is also seen in how Jesus taught this group of men. Mark 6:7-9 reports that Jesus sent the disciples two by two with specific instructions that related to his mission as identified in Luke 4. They went with authority over unclean spirits, calling people to repent. For the disciples, repentance meant changing how people lived, teaming up with all those who follow Jesus in God's New Way of living. There is not a single word about teaching others how Jesus would die for their sins some day in the future.

The disciples were learning that Jesus came teaching a new way of living based on peace, sharing, justice and truth, all basic Torah concepts that promised healing, hope and the potential for new life.

This message is made even more dramatic in Luke 10:1-12 where Jesus expanded the group to seventy persons. The general instructions were much the same with Jesus adding a specific note about teaching content. The counsel is clear: ***"Say to them, the kingdom of God has come near to you".*** That seems to be a summary statement by gospel writers giving the central content of the Jesus message. There is no mention of a future death on the cross.

Evidently for the disciples, and for the gospel writers also, the focus of Jesus during his lifetime was on the presence of God's New Way rather than any theological discussion of salvation through shed blood, suffering and death. The mission of the disciples was to prepare themselves to experience, and then understand, this Jesus message after the teacher was gone.

There is another event that further confirms this role for the disciples. After the resurrection Jesus met with the disciples for forty days (a casual Jewish reference for a long time). It is significant that Jesus used this time to talk with them about God's New Way (Matt.28:19-20).

If the primary mission of Jesus was to die so that God could forgive sinful humanity, this had already been accomplished. One would expect Jesus to use this special time to be absolutely sure that the disciples understood the theological importance of his saving death. This concept of a suffering, dying Messiah was not part of the Jewish Messianic expectation. But Acts 1:3 is quite clear. Jesus used this time to present himself alive to the disciples, and to talk with them about the kingdom of God. This was a traumatic time for the disciples, and to have Jesus use this sacred time to talk about God's New Way indicates the central importance of this theme for Jesus in understanding his own ministry.

5. Luke 4:16-21   Jesus at Nazareth

When he came to Nazareth, where he had been brought up, he went to the Synagogue on the Sabbath day, as was his custom. He stood up to read, and the scroll of the prophet Isaiah was given to him. He unrolled the scroll, and found the place where it was written: "The Spirit of the Lord is upon me, because he has anointed me to bring good news to the poor. He has sent me to proclaim release to the captives and recovery of sight to the blind, to let the oppressed go free, to proclaim the year of the Lord's favor. . . Then he began to say to them, "Today this scripture has been fulfilled in your hearing."

As Luke tells the Jesus story, he looks for a special event that would capture the basic Jesus message as the theme for his gospel. He reports that Jesus received wide general acceptance while teaching in the area synagogues (Luke 4:14-15). But then Luke departs from his normal dependence on Mark's chronology and inserts the story of Jesus returning to his hometown synagogue at Nazareth. Mark's chronology places this story at a more realistic time in the later ministry of Jesus. cf Mark 6:1-6 & Matt. 13:54-58.

Jesus read from Isaiah 61:1-3 which is a declaration of the year of the Lord's favor (the Jubilee year), describing what living in God's new age would be like. It included good news for the poor, release for the captives, recovery of sight for the blind, and freedom for the oppressed. This was not a new message of spiritual salvation to be received some day off in the future, but a declaration of what is happening right now since God's new age is a present reality. By basing his message in Isaiah's Jubilee message, Jesus is saying that this has always been God's intention.

Jesus then used two illustrations showing how God had reached out to Gentiles who then responded positively (the widow at Zarephath, and Naaman the Syrian, both members of enemy nations). This effectively declared that Israel's self assumed status as the elite, privileged people of God did not apply in this new age. All people are to be included in God's New Age. Luke used the violent synagogue reaction to this message as a prophetic indication of what would eventually happen to Jesus. The gospels report several times where Jewish leaders tried to find a way to kill Jesus because they were so angry with what he taught and did (Matt. 12:19, Mk 3:6, Luke 6:11)

When Jesus talked about his mission there was no mention of a new spiritual salvation made possible by his future intention to die on the cross. The Jesus mission was putting in place what had always been God's intention. God's New Way is a call to change how this world functions so that people will not be hungry, or sold into slavery, and even the land will be protected. These elements of human justice were deeply embedded in the Year of Jubilee text which Jesus quoted (Isa. 61:1-3). Jesus saw his mission being a call to Jewish people to obey the original intentions of the Mosaic law and thus be a living expression of God's concern for justice, mercy, and grace (salvation ?) for all people in this life.

Luke sees the death of Jesus not as a salvation event, but as being linked to the content of his preaching the message of God's New Age that was becoming a present reality. Certainly, Luke knew that Jesus had died on the cross, but he does not believe that Jesus came intending to die. Luke sees the message of Jesus as a radical, exciting new reality that challenged the traditional expectations of the people. Rather than accepting this message as a living reality, the religious leadership of that day decided to get rid of the messenger. Jesus sacrificed himself rather than violate the integrity of his relationship with God.

Understandably, there are Christian leaders today who want to spiritualize the content of the Jesus message in this Nazareth sermon. But Jesus was drawing on a specific Year of Jubilee text that was an attempt by ancient Israel to establish justice, equality and mercy in the social, political and economic systems of their day. To say that Jesus is talking about the spiritually blind, or those imprisoned in sin, or that the good news for the poor is a future heavenly salvation is a gross distortion of the message of Jesus calling for life guided by the values of God's New Age.

6. Matthew 5-6-7   The Sermon on the Mount

The Sermon on the Mount is widely accepted as a series of summary statements based on the content of Jesus' teaching ministry. There are those who say that these teachings are not for this life, but are demonstrations of how life will be for those who are fortunate enough to get to heaven. This does not do justice to Jesus. Glenn Stassen, in his book "Just Peacemaking" identifies specific behaviors that Jesus addressed (i.e. killing, adultery, divorce, retaliation, giving alms, swearing falsely, hatred of an enemy, praying, fasting). Stassen says these are very realistic mechanics of bondage that ruin personal relationships and thus have no place in God's New Age. He lists the transforming initiatives that Jesus presented as God's New Way for the people of God and then points out that there is not one word here about a spiritual salvation achieved through the death of Jesus on the cross. Everything in these summaries of statements made by Jesus deals with the healing of human relationships, the lessening of human pain, and the creation of a community in which healing (not war making) is the norm, where sharing generously (not greedy personal accumulation) is the rule, and where an honest yes or no (not intentional deception) builds a community where people trust each other (Stassen pp 44-80).

These faith community's summaries of the teaching of Jesus were written after the crucifixion, yet they make no mention of his death on the cross. It is not faithful to Jesus to shift the focus to include things that were not included in his own presentation of his ministry. We should return to the basic teachings of Jesus for an interpretation of his ministry rather than imposing later theological doctrines that do not reflect what Jesus himself said.

The impact of God's New Way is seen in the wording used in Matthew. There are those who see the text saying there is something blessed about being poor, or meek, or who mourn, or are pure in heart, or are persecuted, or reviled and abused because somehow they will be rewarded in the next life (Matt 5:3-11). But that is a deceptive reading of the text. Why are the poor blessed? God's New Way is here and there are people who will help them and care about them. This is also true for those who mourn. There is nothing sacred or special about being poor, or about mourning or being persecuted. The good news is that that God's New Way is here and people will offer aid, comfort, food, friendship, simply because that is what people do in God's New Way.

The early Anabaptists correctly insisted that the message of Jesus focused on the relationships we have in our daily living because God's New Way is a present reality. They did not ask "Are you saved?" Rather, their focus question was "Are you following Jesus?" They said that the teachings of Jesus were based on the presence of God's New Way, believing that Jesus challenged how we live as his followers. This was a reaction to 15th Century religious beliefs that made Jesus a spiritual sacrifice that restored our relationship to God after we die, thus excusing ourselves from an ethical life based on the core values seen in the life and teachings of Jesus.

The Anabaptists believed the teachings of Jesus are a guide for the way God intends humanity live in this world. They believed God was creating a peaceful world where healing of relationships, meeting human needs of food and health care, and offering comfort for those who are suffering physically or emotionally should become the way followers of Jesus live on a daily basis. It does significant damage to the Jesus message when Jesus is seen primarily as a spiritual rescuer who saves people from this world, assuring them of a new life in a perfect place called heaven.

Dr. Marc Ellis, a Jewish theologian, made a very interesting comparison as he spoke at a Michiana Voices For Middle East Peace public gathering. He identified himself as a teacher of Torah as God's founding guide for ethics and faith in Judaism. Then he said that Christians see Jesus as a teacher of Torah who gave a new interpretation of Torah in the Sermon on the Mount (Matt. 5-7 "you have heard that it hath been said, but I say . . ."). Since Jesus was a Jew who also was a teacher of Torah as the base for faith, there is no reason for Jews and Christians to be at odds with each other. If Christians would stop blaming Jews for the death of Jesus and would follow Jesus with the same seriousness that Jewish people have when they read Torah, we would discover that we have a lot in common, and we could work together doing the things of God. (Ellis, MV4MEP, 11/10/2017).

7. Matthew 11:2-16   Jesus answers John the Baptist

> ***When John heard in prison what the Messiah was doing, he sent word by his disciples; and said to him, "Are you the one who is to come, or are we to wait for another?" Jesus answered them, "Go and tell John what you hear and see; the blind receive their sight, the lame walk, the lepers are cleansed, the deaf hear, the dead are raised, and the poor have the good news brought to them. And blessed is anyone who takes no offense at me."***

John the Baptist was a fresh voice in the Jewish religious world and his message of repentance attracted a lot of attention. Herod arrested John for making critical statements about Herod's immoral behavior. While John was in prison Jesus began his own active ministry, and this raised serious questions for John. The First Century Jewish religious community had a set of theological expectations about the promised Messiah, and some of them had political, military implications for power and national control. Jesus, however, patterned his ministry after the Servant model of Isaiah. John, locked in prison, wondered whether Jesus really was the Messiah they were looking for because his ministry style did not fit with the popular expectations.

So messengers came to Jesus from John, asking rather bluntly, *"Are you the one who is to come, or should we look for someone else?"* (If you are the Messiah, why aren't you doing what we know the Messiah will do?) It is a classic question asking Jesus to self-identify, and then prove it by what he was doing. It is not often that Jesus was asked a question with that specificity.

How Jesus chose to answer John helps us understand Jesus. Rather than a simple "YES", Jesus asked John to look at the evidence and then decide. Jesus gave this supporting evidence: *"the blind receive their sight, the lame walk, the lepers are cleansed, the deaf hear, the dead are raised, and the poor have the good news brought to them".* It is precisely what Jesus identified as his mission when he quoted from Isaiah at Nazareth (Isa 58:6-7 & 61:1-3), and it was an honest report of what Jesus was doing.

But something is missing. Why did Jesus not tell John, "I have come to preach the good news of salvation that I will provide by dying on the cross to appease God's anger with humanity so that by believing in me they might be saved?" That is the validation most contemporary Christians use to prove that Jesus was the Messiah. If ever there was a time when Jesus could have made a declaration about his intention to die on the cross, this would have been it. Yet he made no mention of that idea. Could it be that coming to die was not part of his original mission?

A faithful response would accept the answer that Jesus gave. It is a clear statement in which Jesus reports exactly what he was doing. And if that is what Jesus said he came to do, that should be what those who follow Jesus are doing today. It is not valid to use a ministry description for Jesus that Jesus did not use for himself?

Jesus ended his explanation for John with what might be seen as a rather sharp rebuke. *"Blessed is anyone who takes no offense at me."* (Blessed are those who understand that this incarnation of God's New Age is what the Messiah is all about.) The answer implies, "John, I expect this evidence will effectively answer your question." Faithfulness to Jesus asks that we also accept Jesus' own explanation of his messianic mission, and then discover what it means for us to be 'followers of Jesus' in our own lives.

8. Matthew 25:31-46   At the Judgment Seat

"When the Son of Man comes in his glory, and all the angels with him, then he will sit on the throne of his glory. All the nations will be gathered before him and he will separate people one from another as a shepherd separates the sheep from the goats...

Then the king will say to those at his right hand, 'Come you that are blessed by my Father, inherit the kingdom prepared for you from the foundation of the world; for I was hungry and you gave me food, I was thirsty and you gave me something to drink, I was a stranger and you welcomed me, I was naked and you gave me clothing, I was sick and you took care of me, I was in prison and you visited me'. Then the righteous will answer him, 'Lord, when was it that we saw you hungry and gave you food, or thirsty and gave you something to drink? And when was it that we saw you a stranger and welcomed you, or naked and gave you clothing? And when was it that we saw you sick or in prison and visited you?"

And the king will answer them, "Truly I tell you, just as you did it to one of the least of these who are members of my family, you did it to me."

Then he will say to those at his left hand, 'you who are accursed, depart from me into the eternal fire prepared for the devil and his angels; for I was hungry and you gave me no food, I was thirsty and you gave me nothing to drink, I was a stranger and you did not welcome me, naked and you did not give me clothing, sick and in prison and you did not visit me.'

Then they will also answer, 'Lord, when was it that we saw you hungry or thirsty or a stranger or naked or sick or in prison, and did not take care of you?' Then he will answer them, "Truly I tell you, just as you did not do it to one of the least of these, you did not do it to me.' And these will go away into eternal punishment, but the righteous into eternal life.

Matthew presents a dramatic story using the imagery of how decisions will be made regarding eternal life. The Son of Man is on the throne, and all the nations of the world are gathered around him. One group is warmly welcomed into God's presence, while another group is summarily dismissed.

The standard explanation is that Christians are the ones who will be welcomed because they believe the right things about Jesus. Unfortunately, in this system, those who do not claim Jesus as Lord will be refused entry. The Christian mission is to tell these people about how Jesus died for them so they might believe in him and not be excluded from their heavenly reward.

But that is not how the biblical story is told. It is almost humorous in its Jewish story telling pattern. One group is invited to enter God's presence, and the reason given is that they fed the hungry, gave the thirsty a drink, welcomed the stranger, clothed the naked, took care of the sick, and visited prisoners--- all things identified with the ministry of Jesus.

But these people, who are identified as righteous, are bewildered because they have no memory of doing any of these things for Jesus. They are told that when they did these things for others, it was as though they did them for him, even though they were not aware of what they were doing. They are welcomed into God's eternal kingdom (since they were already living God's New Way).

The second group is labelled "accursed" and are turned away. Obviously, this is not what they were expecting and they are angry. Their defense is that if they had only known it was Jesus, they certainly would have done all these things for him. It is not a major jump to imagine them as being pious persons who felt they were doing all the right things. They attended synagogue worship on a regular basis, they studied Torah, and even gave an alms offering on special occasions. It is easy to fit them comfortably into the Good Samaritan story as ones who passed by on the other side while on their way to worship.

The explanation they receive is virtually identical to that given the first group. I was there, in all these persons who were needing help, but you did nothing for them. You create excuses for your lack of compassion, but you did nothing. Therefore, I will have nothing to do with you.

The imagery is interesting, but the point of the story is vivid. Salvation (experiencing God's grace) is found in being the presence of God as we relate to others in the world in which we live. Acting with compassion and mercy for others is being the presence of Jesus in this world where God is present in the life and experience of every human being. There is no mention of regular participation in worship, of believing the right things, or even knowing that Jesus died to save them from their sins. This becomes especially important because their sin was simply that they did not show God's love and compassion for persons who were in need. They were not living God's New Way. This was not just an innocent oversight on a busy day. It was a denial of God's presence, reflecting the story Jesus told about the two religious leaders in the Good Samaritan story who were denying God's concern for others as they passed by on the other side.

The heart of this story is that if we want to find God, we should look around us, in the faces of every person with whom we share life. How we treat others is an indication of our own awareness of God's presence with us, and of our own level of gratitude for God's grace and forgiveness already received.

Several things need to be noted. One cannot argue that this is a reward, or an "earned salvation" based on what we do for others. The people who were invited in had no expectations about receiving any merit for what they had done. They were not acting in mercy with the anticipation that God would be watching and would reward them for what they had done. They simply saw a human need and gave whatever help they could give. In simple language they were living God's New Way without consciously being aware of it. They are proof that living God's New Way not only shares a blessing with others, but it also returns a blessing to you, even though you were not trying to earn it by what you did.

The second concern is that there is no mention of any doctrinal belief system about Jesus having died on the cross as being the controlling factor for entry into God's eternal presence. This says that teaching doctrinal beliefs to hungry people without doing something about their hunger is a denial of God's presence with us, and shows our ignorance about God's concern for other persons.

As Matthew tells the story, the message of salvation is seen in how we respond to others as we live in God's New Age. Jesus focused on a shared response to God's desire for new life, for healing and mercy for all people, rather than doctrinal beliefs that allows persons to separate themselves from those who are hungry, thirsty, poor, sick, or in prison.

In a religious world where right doctrinal beliefs about Jesus provide the only possible entryway into God's eternal presence, it does seem important to note that the gospel writers effectively ignored that idea as they wrote about how judgment will be determined for entry into God's presence. This challenges us to rethink our own beliefs about God and how God views humanity.

9. Luke 19:1-10   New Life for Zacchaeus

He entered Jericho and was passing through it. A man was there named Zacchaeus; he was a tax collector and was rich . . . .He was a short man, so he climbed a sycamore tree to see Jesus. When Jesus got to the tree he looked up and said to him, "Zacchaeus, come down. Today is my day to be a guest in your home. . . . (After supper, Zacchaeus and Jesus came outside Zacchaeus's home). . *.Zacchaeus just stood there, a little stunned. He stammered apologetically, "Master, I give away half my income to the poor---and if I'm caught cheating, I will pay four times the damages." Jesus said, "Today is the day of salvation in this home! Here is Zacchaeus, son of Abraham! For the son of man came to find and restore the lost". (Peterson, The Message)*

Luke opened the public ministry of Jesus with a visit to his hometown of Nazareth where he read from a text in Isaiah, and talked about the Year of Jubilee (Lk 4:16-30). The Jewish people who were in the synagogue responded with rejection. Luke ends the public ministry of Jesus by telling several stories which demonstrate a striking contrast in how people responded to the Good News that Jesus was teaching.

First there is a wealthy Jewish leader who came to Jesus asking how he might inherit the eternal life that Jesus has been talking about. The response of Jesus is very instructive. He says nothing about believing the right things.

He instructed the man to "*sell what you have, give to the poor*, (become involved in acts of social justice) *and you will have what you are asking for*". But the man rejected the answer Jesus gave because he was rich (Lk. 18:18-25).

Then Luke has two stories that contrast this "rejection response" with the positive responses of two persons who were not socially accepted. A blind man pleads for help and his sight was restored (see Luke 4:18 where Jesus promised "recovery of sight to the blind"), Lk 18:35-43. In that day, blind persons were not permitted in the temple. In God's New Age things will be different. Blind people will no longer be excluded.

Then there is Zacchaeus, a tax collector. Jesus invited himself to eat with Zacchaeus. There is no record of what they talked about, but Luke reports that after the meal Zacchaeus announced that he was going to live by God's New Way. He would give away half of his wealth, and make restitution "IF I have defrauded anyone". **IF** I have defrauded anyone! Everyone knew that most tax collectors got rich by defrauding people, and we are told that Zacchaeus was rich!

The response of Jesus is important. "Today, salvation has come to this house". Zacchaeus has changed (repented?). Jesus announced salvation 'today' because this man is now committing himself to live the way every son of Abraham should live. His salvation had nothing to do withwhat he will need to believe about what is going to happen to Jesus next week. But it has everything to do with his decision to live by God's values instead of the Roman rules that guided tax collectors. Zacchaeus indeed had been lost to the ways of God, but in his acceptance of God's New Way he was "born again" and salvation (new life?) had come to his house.

Zacchaeus did not earn his salvation by giving away half of his wealth. But in giving away half of his wealth he discovered a new reality that was there waiting for him to accept. Imagine the excitement for both Zacchaeus and his neighbors when he showed up at their door saying "I want to apologize, and give you a refund on your taxes from last year." Go back again to the message of Jesus in Luke 4 "*he has appointed me to bring good news to the poor.*" Luke understands that God's New Way does work in the lives of people just as Jesus said it would.

10. Mark 11:11, 15-19   The "Cleansing" of the Temple

Then he entered Jerusalem and went into the temple, and when he had looked around at everything, as it was already late, he went out to Bethany with the twelve... On the following day...they came to Jerusalem. And he entered the temple and began to drive out those who were selling and those who were buying in the temple, and he overturned the tables of the money changers and the seats of those who sold doves; and he would not allow anyone to carry anything through the temple. He was teaching and saying, "Is it not written, 'my house shall be called a house of prayer for all the nations'? But you have made it a den of robbers."

When the chief priests and scribes heard it, they kept looking for a way to kill him; for they were afraid of him, because the whole crowd was spellbound by his teaching.

Mark 11 and John 2 both tell a story normally referred to as the "cleansing of the temple". It is the most dramatic action taken by Jesus in his three year public ministry. Historically, it has raised problems for pacifist groups because people often focus on the "violence" that Jesus used to make a theological point. This raises a secondary question of whether the non-lethal force used on the animals or on the tables of the money changers is ever permitted for the Christians. The text is precise. Jesus upset the tables used by those who were changing money, and used an improvised whip of cords to drive out the cattle. This is not what most pacifists would consider 'lethal force' or a violation of their commitment to the way of peace. There is no threat to human life or safety. But arguing this point effectively distorts the theological point that Jesus is making.

This is a critical event for the gospel writers. It is one of the few stories told in all four gospels. John sees it as a significant signpost in understanding the mission of Jesus. He moves it from the last week of Jesus' life (where it appears in the synoptic gospels), and places it very early during the first weeks of Jesus' ministry. John says that the cleansing of the temple occurred during the first experience of Passover for Jesus. It is widely accepted that John focused on theological meaning rather than chronological details. Thus,

Mark's timing is preferred, placing this event during the last week of Jesus' life.

John's decision to move this dramatic event to the first Passover visit by Jesus makes a serious statement about how the ministry of Jesus was in sharp contrast with the worship practices in the temple. This also includes criticism of the theology of the Jewish rabbis who controlled the temple. It is important to look at the event itself before returning to John's basic theological message.

Mark gives one important bit of information. In Mark 11:11 *Jesus went into the temple; and when he had looked around at everything, as it was already late, he went out to Bethany with the twelve.* The next day (11:12 & 15) he went back to the temple and upset the tables of the money-changers, and drove out the cattle and sheep. This action by Jesus was not an impulsive act of violence. It had a specific theological intent and purpose. When the Jewish leaders asked Jesus to tell them why he did this, Jesus explained: *"This is to be a house of prayer for all nations, and you have made it a den of robbers"* (Matt. 21:13).

What was the nature of temple worship that Jesus found so repulsive? It is often claimed that this involved economic abuse with money changers overcharging for their services, plus the selling of cattle or sheep for sacrifices. But the central issue is far more spiritual than economic.

By the first century sacrifice had become the centerpiece of temple worship. People who were honestly concerned about their relationship with God were being taught that killing (even if 'only' an innocent animal) was the way to achieve forgiveness and reconciliation with God. This raises the serious question whether sacrifice was ever God's intended method of reconciliation.

Originally, in Old Testament stories, when two persons had a quarrel they were to resolve the issue, then share a meal together in celebration of their reconciliation. The community joined with them in this meal of celebration. An animal was killed not as a sacrifice, but for a feast in celebration of the reconciliation that had been achieved, not as the agent of that reconciliation. (See Gen. 31:53-55)

Centuries later Solomon built the temple in Jerusalem and explicitly identified it as a place for prayer and forgiveness. *"Hear the plea of your servant and of your people Israel when they pray toward this place; hear in heaven, your dwelling place, heed and forgive." (II Chr. 6:19-20).* This is followed by twelve statements saying that people, both Israelites and foreigners, will come to this place *"to pray and plead with you in this house, then hear from heaven, forgive the sin of your people Israel."* The same statement is made on behalf of the foreigner, *"when a foreigner comes and prays toward this house, then hear in heaven and do all that the foreigner asks of you. . ." (6:32-33).*

Solomon described the temple as a place of prayer and forgiveness for all people. But the imagery was immediately muddled in II Chr. 7:5 where Solomon began an enormous sacrifice of 22,000 oxen and 120,000 sheep in gratitude to God for giving Israel the temple and for hearing their prayers. It is clearly stated that this was an act of celebration and dedication, but it is understandable to see how, centuries later, the tradition might interpret the event differently.

There is an unusual incident reported in I Kings 8:10-11 about what happened in the midst of this enormous sacrificial slaughter of animals. *"As the priests came out of the inner holy sanctuary, a cloud filled the Temple of the Lord. The priests could not continue their work because the glorious presence of the Lord filled the Temple."* The presence of smoke was often identified as being the presence of God (Ex. 19:18, Isa. 4:5). Solomon's prayer called for God to be present in this sacred temple. The smoke could be interpreted as God actually responding to Solomon's plea. But it might also be seen that God's presence, forcing a temporary stop to the priestly slaughter, was a statement of disapproval of the whole sacrificial process? Being a house of prayer for all nations met with God's approval, but the sacrifice of innocent animals was a very different thing, and God effectively stopped the practice (at least temporarily).

This confusion over the role of sacrifice is addressed by the prophets.

Hosea 6:6 *"I desire mercy and not sacrifice, knowledge of God rather than burnt offerings."*

Micah 6:8 *"With what shall I come before the Lord, and bow myself before God on high? Shall I come with burnt offerings, with calves a year old? Will the Lord be pleased with thousands of rams, with ten thousands of rivers of* oil? Shall I give my firstborn for my transgression, the fruit of my body for the sin of my soul? He has told you, O mortal, what is good, and what does the Lord require of you. Do justice, love kindness, and walk humbly with your God."

Isaiah 1:11 *"What to me is the multitude of your sacrifices? I have had enough of burnt offerings of rams, and the fat of fed beasts. I do not delight in the blood of bulls, or of lambs, or of goats. . . . bringing offerings is futile, incense is an abomination to me. . .learn to do good, seek justice, rescue the oppressed, defend the orphan, plead for the widow."*

Amos 5:22,24 *"Even though you offer me your burnt offerings. . .I will not accept them, and the offerings of well-being of your fatted animals I will not look upon. . .but let justice roll down like waters and righteousness like an ever-flowing stream."*

The Old Testament prophets had a deeply felt concern about the developing institution of sacrifice as required for reconciliation with God. Over the generations, the belief in reconciliation by sacrifice was gaining in acceptance by the religious leadership. Gradually it became commonly accepted that if you sinned, offer a sacrifice. God will smell the incense of the burnt offering and will know that you are sorry for what you have done. You will be forgiven by God without ever having to deal directly with God or the person against whom you sinned. Sacrifices became a ritual to receive forgiveness rather than being a celebration of forgiveness that had been received.

By the First Century CE, sacrifices had become the standard ritual for persons to make peace with God, and the temple did a thriving business in animal sacrifice. The temple was now a place where foreign money was exchanged for local money to buy a lamb or a calf which would be sacrificed, providing assurance of forgiveness even though there had been no contact with God in any accountable way. There was no need to repent, or to change the way one lived because you had done what God required of you (according to the sacrificial theology of the temple leadership).

This is what Jesus was objecting to---the concept that God requires blood and death in order to forgive. This temple ritual was blasphemy before God. Jesus was protesting the basic message of temple sacrifice and the issue of how one relates to God. Jubilee living in God's New Age had become a rejected bit of ancient history. The Old Testament prophets repeatedly declared that God wanted righteous living, not animal sacrifices. If blood sacrifice was not God's way for humanity to find reconciliation with God, we should not assume that God sent Jesus to be a blood sacrifice for the sins of humanity. This is a clear rejection of prophetic statements about what God requires for humanity to experience forgiveness, healing and reconciliation.

If Jesus truly represented the presence and will of God, he was right in protesting the practice of sacrifice in the temple. But it raises a serious question. Would God demand the sacrificial death of Jesus if a sacrificial death is not what God requires in order to grant forgiveness? Were Hosea, Micah, Amos, and Isaiah wrong when they said that God wants righteous living instead of blood sacrifices? We distort the heart of God's message of love and forgiveness by continuing to insist that Jesus was a blood sacrifice demanded by God so that humanity could be forgiven.

11. Matthew 28:18-20   The Great Commission

Jesus came and said to them. "All authority in heaven and on earth has been given to me. Go therefore and make disciples of all nations, baptizing them in the name of the Father, and of the Son, and of the Holy Spirit, teaching them to obey everything that I have commanded you. And remember, I am with you always, to the end of the age.

The final instructions given by Jesus to the disciples have critical importance because in them, Jesus explains what his followers should do when he is no longer with them. Most Christians learned these instructions years ago, yet the content of these final instructions eludes us.

The church most often reads these instructions as saing "Go into all the world and preach the gospel, telling people they will be saved if they believe that I died for them on the cross." But a simple reading of the text will not permit that translation. The text gives a very different and rather specific set of instructions: *"Go and make disciples of all nations . . teaching them to obey everything that I have commanded you and I will be with you always."*

Jesus tells the disciples they should go throughout the world inviting people to join in living God's New Way. The message is clear. They are instructed to continue spreading the message of Jesus. Nothing is said about proclaiming the theological significance of his death on the cross. Jesus is telling the disciples to share with everyone God's New Way just as he had shared it with them. But modern Christianity has altered the content of the gospel from being a call to God's new way of living, and has made it a system of believing right doctrinal facts about the birth and then the death of Jesus on the cross. This passes over the life of Jesus and implies that what Jesus taught has little importance, saying it is the death of Jesus, not his teachings, that matters.

But when the Great Commission is read carefully, Jesus is telling the disciples that the message to be shared with others is the same message he shared with them. Thus, Jesus places the focus of the gospel on the content of his life and teachings, not on a sacrificial death on the cross.

In the Great Commission, Jesus reverses the Isaiah message in Isa. 2:3-4 *"Many people shall come and say, 'Come, let us go up to the mountain of the Lord, to the house of the God of Jacob; that he may teach us his ways and that we may walk in his paths. For out of Zion shall go forth instruction, and the word of the Lord from Jerusalem. He shall judge between the nations, and shall arbitrate for many people; they shall beat their swords into plowshares, and their spears into pruning hooks; nation shall not lift up sword against nation, neither shall they learn war any more."* (This same message is found in Micah 4:1-2.)

Jesus instructed the disciples not to wait for the nations to come to them. They were to take God's Jubilee message of peace and wholeness to the nations, emphasizing that this is not a message to be preserved for ourselves, but it is God's universal message intended for all nations and all peoples, in all places, for all time. This picks up the theme of God's call to Abraham: "in you all the nations of the earth will be blessed" (Gen. 12:3). God's vision for the salvation of all people in all nations is picked up by Jesus and shared with the disciples. Being the last words of Jesus, these final instructions given to the disciples continue to have relevance for us today.

How many refugees today would experience salvation in the Jesus meaning of the word if the church would be an active agent of peace and healing rather than engaging in divisive condemnation of other religions as we call them to be converted to our system of theological doctrine rather than to God's way of living. This is what the Pharisees did, and Jesus had harsh words of condemnation on them for doing it. ***Woe to you scribes and Pharisees, hypocrites! For you cross sea and land to make a single convert, and you make the new convert twice as much a child of hell as yourselves!*** (Matt. 23:15). In his lifetime Jesus did not focus on right doctrinal thinking about God, but on God's compassionate caring for others as demonstrated in his own ministry.

Unfortunately, much of Protestant Christianity continues to insist on right doctrinal beliefs about Jesus as the basis for salvation rather than a faith commitment to follow the teachings of Jesus in caring for others. This is the most dangerous heresy to hit Christian Faith in over a thousand years. Yet it continues to be the dominant way of thinking for many Christians in North America. It distorts the Jesus message by focusing on something that God has done for us (often exclusively for us), rather than the Jesus call for all humanity to share an active compassionate ministry that sacrifices one's own self in caring for others.

Staying with the Biblical language of Jesus helps us understand this dilemma. Salvation is a present experience in our own lives as we respond to the message of Jesus inviting us to live in the blessing of God's New Way. It is not something external that God provides for us by having Jesus die on the cross as a sacrifice to atone for our sins. Evangelism involves being a living expression of all that Jesus was in his lifetime, inviting others to join with us in being people of God's New Age living in peace, with hope, offering healing and mercy to everyone around us. Salvation is not something special that God has done just for us who believe the right things about Jesus. Rather, salvation is something we share in right now as we live in the grace of God giving incarnational expression to the teachings of Jesus. Salvation is not something we hope to get some day in the future. Salvation is the condition of God's presence in which we now live each day of our lives.

12. Acts 13:28-31   Diversity in Telling the Story?

The four gospel accounts of the life of Jesus do not report every statement or event in exactly the same way. Some details in the story are different, and sometimes the basic content of the story as told by Matthew differs from how Luke tells the same story. Even more difficult, sometimes a statement of Jesus reported by Matthew in one setting appears to conflict with something Matthew reports Jesus saying in a different setting.

The gospel writers lived in a religious culture that was primarily oral. As stories about Jesus were shared within the gathered community over a 40 year period, it is inevitable that not every story would be told in exactly the same way. The early faith community did not seem to be bothered by this. They told the stories without arguing among themselves over which version of the story was the accurate one. The theme of the story and their response to that theme had priority over internal debates about which story best reported what Jesus actually said.

This shows that the early faith community was comfortable living together with multiple versions of the same story. It is commonly accepted that Mark was the first writer to record an account of these stories. The evidence indicates that both Matthew and Luke had a copy of Mark when they wrote their own record of the actions and sayings of Jesus, because they copied nearly one third of Mark directly into their own accounts of the ministry of Jesus. There were other stories from the life of Jesus that were rejected by the early church because their bizarre nature did not reflect the same sense of authenticity, nor did they reflect the best community memory of what Jesus had said or done. Some of these stories appear in the later apocryphal gospels that were rejected by the early faith communities.

But the question is still critical. How does one explain the conflicting versions of a given saying by Jesus? How does one decide which one has the best accurate authenticity? This did not seem to be a problem for the early church leadership because they permitted these versions to co-exist side by side even when the content was different. Only much later in history did Biblical scholars detect there might be a problem to be resolved. That resolution involves a study of what we know about the person telling the story and how the story was told. An example is what Jesus said in his last meeting with the disciples.

Matthew 28:19-20: ***"go therefore and make disciples of all nations, baptizing them. . . . and teaching them to obey everything I have commanded you."*** Luke reports this differently: ***"And he said to them, thus it is written, that the Messiah is to suffer and to rise from the dead on the third day, and that repentance and forgiveness of sins is to be proclaimed in his name to all nations, beginning from Jerusalem."*** (Luke 24:46-47).

The difference in the two accounts is significant. Matthew calls for making disciples, baptizing them and teaching others the same content that he had taught them with no reference to his suffering, death, or resurrection. But Luke identifies Jesus' suffering, and rising from the dead, then proclaims repentance and forgiveness in his name. Each of these texts is a legitimate scripture and should be taken seriously, yet they do not say the same thing. So how does one determine which account should have priority in understanding what Jesus told the disciples?

Matthew was one of the disciples and would have been present with the eleven when these instructions were given, so that would seem to give his account priority. Also, his focus on what Jesus taught dominates his gospel account. Implied in this challenge to baptize and teach is the assumption that these teachings will lead to repentance and change in how one lives.

Luke was also a committed follower of Jesus, but his path to faith was quite different from what Matthew experienced. Luke never met or heard Jesus in person, and he was not part of the disciple group that met with Jesus after the resurrection. Luke learned about Jesus from Paul at least fifteen to twenty years after the death of Jesus, so his interpretation of things Jesus said would reflect the same community memories that shaped Paul's understanding. There is an overlap in these two statements regarding repentance and forgiveness. The difference is that Luke links this change to the suffering and resurrection of Jesus, while Matthew connects repentance and forgiveness with the things Jesus taught during his lifetime.

Both of these accounts have a common theme of repentance and change in how one lives, but they also represent different strands in how the life/death/resurrection of Jesus was understood within the early Christian community. It is not helpful to argue whether one version is accurate and the other is wrong, but it does lead to the observation that Matthew's language and content more closely reflects what Jesus taught throughout his earthly ministry. Thus it seems appropriate to give priority to the Matthean version without discrediting the Lukan account.

This would also apply to other settings in Luke and Acts where the traditional language of suffering, repentance and forgiveness is used. Jesus often forgave persons for deeds in their past, and challenged them to live by the values of God's New Way. Forgiveness assures God's grace for all who turn from a life dominated by the values of the world toward a new life guided by God's New Way.

There is another text which helps explain these differing memories within the faith community. In Acts 13:28-31, 39 Paul is in Antioch in Pisidia explaining to a Jewish audience how the death of Jesus happened. ***"Even though they found no cause for a sentence of death, they asked Pilate to have him killed. When they had carried out everything that was written about him, they took him down from the tree and laid him in a tomb. But God raised him from the dead."***

In talking about Jesus with this Jewish audience, Paul draws on two different memory traditions, bringing together the innocence of Jesus and unidentified scriptures in the Old Testament. In a Jewish setting where sacrificial language would have been well accepted, Paul chose to avoid that language and focus instead on the involvement of God in raising Jesus from the dead. Here Paul affirms that the death of Jesus was an illegitimate act by Rome to solve a political/religious problem that did not really exist. He also said that God reversed that decision by raising Jesus from the dead. Paul is confronting his audience with a choice. You can either accept the Roman version of what happened, or the Christian understanding of how God changed history. For Paul, the choice was obvious. The resurrection was God's rejection of a bad Roman decision, and that dramatically changes how you view Jesus of Nazareth.

This confirms that Paul believed the crucifixion of Jesus was not a preplanned God event to save humanity, but was Rome's reaction when they felt threatened by the life and message of Jesus. This was how the early faith community told the story of what happened that terrible weekend, and Paul repeats that explanation for his Jewish audience.

From the gospel writers, and from Paul adapting the various memory traditions in the early faith community, we can learn how to live together without having to argue with, or separate ourselves from, persons who read the details differently from how we see the story being told. Inevitably we will have differing preferences, but if we can affirm our common commitment to Jesus as Lord, accept our human differences, and determine to share together as faithful followers of Jesus, we will be people of new life and a blessing to those who live among us.

III. Did Jesus Have to Die?

When one moves into this understanding of Jesus and the salvation of humanity, the obvious question is 'Why did Jesus die?' Was it God's eternal plan that Jesus had to die, so that God could see the blood, God's honor would be satisfied, and God could then forgive? That is the classic Substitutionary Atonement theory which many Christians hold to be the only correct Biblical explanation for the death of Jesus. But this explanation does not fit with the words of Jesus. It is a much later heresy that violates the person, mission, and message of Jesus. It also does significant damage to how people understand the basic nature of God.

Substitutionary Atonement language is not used by Jesus when talking about his own life and ministry. Substitutionary Atonement says that God sent Jesus to die as a substitute for us so that God could forgive our sins. This theological belief system says someone had to die in order to maintain the moral balance of the universe. There has to be a penalty for sinful behavior, so Jesus (who was sinless) took our place, paying the price of death, thus making it possible for God to forgive humanity.

If it is true that the death of Jesus is God's saving act, then that act, by itself, has to be effective for all humanity, not just believing Christians. But immediately those who cling most tightly to this belief will object, saying that in order for the death of Jesus to save them, each person has to accept it and believe it. It is valid only for those who believe this is what Jesus did, for without belief there is no salvation. But if one must believe in order to be saved, then that belief becomes the ultimate saving factor, not the death itself.

This creates two immediate problems. If the death of Jesus is an act of God to save humanity, then that act effectively saves all humanity. That is Universalism which most Christians quickly reject. If faith in that death is required, then salvation is achieved by that act of believing, which is something every person has to do for themselves. That is an expression of salvation by personal works, which is also rejected by most Christians on the basis of Paul's counsel in Ephesians 2:8-9. *for by grace you have been saved through faith, and this is not your own doing; it is the gift of God---not the result of works, so no one can boast.* When Paul talks about "faith" he is trusting that Jesus was telling the truth about God and what God wills for humanity.

In this situation the Biblical language used by Jesus is preferable. Salvation is not something external that God provided for us by having Jesus die on the cross as an atoning sacrifice for sin. It is not something special just for the select few who believe the right doctrinal things about Jesus. Salvation is not something we get, it is the reality in which we live in grateful response to God's grace shared so freely with us.

Jesus did not come from God with explicit instructions that his mission was to die for our sins. God never intended sacrifices to deal with the consequences of sinfulness. Jesus did not die on the cross to change how God thinks about humanity. Jesus came to change how humanity thinks about God. The message of Jesus calls us to live in harmony with a God who by very nature is loving and merciful, who invites us to live freely in God's New Age. This understanding says that Jesus, in the tradition of the Biblical prophets, is calling for a return to a way of living patterned upon God's original, and eternal, intentions for all humanity.

But this new way of thinking severely threatened the religious and political leaders of his day. They saw Jesus as a challenge to their power and control of both their religious and political systems. Their solution to the problem was to squelch the message by getting rid of the messenger. Thus Jesus died because of his commitment to remain faithful to God's mission as teacher of God's New Way rather than sacrifice the message in order to protect his own life.

Thus it is possible to see the death of Jesus as a sacrifice. But it was a sacrifice made by Jesus, not one pre-designed by God long before it happened. The choice that Jesus had is seen in his response in the garden of Gethsemane (Matt. 26:51-53). Peter had just used his sword in an attempt to defend Jesus against the soldiers who had come to arrest him. Jesus told Peter, *Do you not think that I cannot appeal to my Father, and he will at once*

send me more than twelve legions? A Roman legion was 6,000 men, so this would be 72,000 angels, which was nearly twice the number of Roman soldiers stationed in all of Israel ! Rather than call on the Father to save him at this critical moment, Jesus made a choice—to stay with the integrity of his own teaching and not resort to angelic military might to save his own life. This choice was one of several steps that ultimately led to his death.

Just prior to this challenge by Judas, Jesus had been praying. Three times he prayed for strength, pleading with God, asking if there might be another way (Matt. 26:36-46). This raises the question whether his death was really part of God's original plan for Jesus' ministry. If Jesus had known that his mission on earth was to die for the sins of humanity, it is extremely unlikely that he would, at this last minute, be asking for a change in the mission.

A compromise at this point might have saved his life, but it would have meant a denial of everything he had been teaching and all the things he had done in demonstration of God's New Way. Do you love your enemies until that enemy is standing in front of you with a sword in his hand? In this situation Jesus prayed for strength, not deliverance or protection.

This same message is seen the next day when Jesus had been tried, convicted, and sentenced to death. He is now on the cross, and his humanness bursts out in a dramatic cry **"My God, My God, Why have you forsaken me**? (Matt., 17:46). If Jesus had come with the clear intention of dying, this cry makes no sense because by his death God's perfect will was being achieved. It is more likely that in this horrific situation Jesus is saying, *"I can understand the disciples leaving me, I can even understand Peter denying he ever knew me, but dear God, why have YOU forsaken me, leaving me here alone to die. In this moment when I need you most—where are you?"* (Who among us has not uttered that same cry at least once in our lives?)

Once again, this cry says that the death of Jesus was the result of his living and teaching a new way that challenged the religious and political structures of his day. These authorities responded in their typical way of problem solving by killing the messenger. This 'kill the messenger' response has been repeated time and time again by modern world leaders who seem to be incapable of learning the futility of this approach. There were the martyrs in the early church. There were 16th Century Anabaptists who had to choose between recanting their faith, or dying for their faith. More recent examples are Dr. Martin Luther King, Michael Sharp, Keija Martin, Kayla Mueller, Shama & Shehzad Masih. Political leaders still kill people who dare to challenge their way of thinking about God, about Truth, or about how they rule over others..

In this experience of death, Jesus was confirming again his commitment to everything he had been teaching about God and God's New Way. Faithfulness to God does not automatically guarantee a long and comfortable life. Jesus demonstrated that by accepting death at the hands of the forces of evil. It was not the original plan when he began his ministry, but his actions demonstrate his own commitment to the Father and to the rightness of the Father's way, for even death does not negate the validity of God's New Age. His response to the national and religious authorities of his day is the personal incarnation of everything he had been preaching for three years. Personal integrity and commitment to God were at the core of who Jesus was.

Where did this idea that God sent Jesus as a sacrifice for human sin originate? The Saducees controlled the temple and they would not have supported most of how Jesus interpreted the law or how he included sinful persons in his friendship circle. Paul's Pharisaic background taught him that righteousness came through prayer and righteous living under the law (Torah). Thus, he probably did not fully approve of what Jesus did in the temple, but his response would have been less hostile than was the reaction of the temple priests. But after his conversion he faced the dilemma of how to explain the death of Jesus in a religious culture that had sacrifice at its center.

To do that, Paul redefined Jesus, moving him from being a prophet teacher of Torah who challenged the standard Pharisaic application of the law, and made him into a divine sacrifice given by God that made all other sacrifices unnecessary. Thus the death of Jesus had salvific meaning because it was God's ultimate act of redemption.

Paul's Pharisaic beliefs that God was in control of history had been challenged by Stephen's recital before the Sanhedrin telling how Israel had often defied God's activity in history (Acts 7). Paul needed to show how the crucifixion of Jesus was actually a statement of God's presence in history. This was made more difficult by an Old Testament text in Deut. 21:23:

"anyone who is hung on a tree is under God's curse". With Paul's intense theological training in Torah, one can understand how the death of Jesus on the cross had to be resolved in order for the message of Jesus to be accepted. Paul had to remove the stigma of centuries of religious thinking and establish a new explanation that made this death an act of divine intervention. Paul also had to address the concerns held by Deuteronomy quoting Jewish rabbis, and at the same time remove the Roman explanation that death by crucifixion was due to crimes against the Roman state.

Paul does not address the broader theological issue of negating salvation by blood sacrifice. Instead he chose to establish the divine status of Jesus' death being an expression of God's presence in human history. It is an understandable attempt, but unfortunately it does not deal with how Jesus understood his own life and death. It helps to recognize that Paul had no contact with Jesus as a teacher during Jesus' lifetime, so he could not have asked Jesus about the place of the cross in his own messianic ministry. Paul developed this understanding in his three years of wrestling with his theological training before returning to Jerusalem where he met with Peter for two weeks (Gal. 1:18). That task, in itself, was no small challenge. As he studied Old Testament scriptures, he faced the serious task of integrating the crucifixion of Jesus into his belief that God is in control of history.

Paul died nearly ten years before any of the gospels were written so he had no first hand written evidence to shape his thinking. He knew only the stories that were being told by the faith community. Thus the issue of how much Paul influenced the developing faith of the early church, and how much that growing faith influenced Paul is an open debate.

But it is hard to overstate the impact Paul had as the primary theological teacher for that early decade of faith development. He had a critical influence at the first Jerusalem Conference (Acts 15), and with his profound commitment to Jesus as Lord, he shaped the missionary life of the faith community reaching from Jerusalem up into Asia Minor, to Greece, and finally to Rome. His experience with the risen Lord on the Damascus Road convinced Paul that Jesus was the promised Messiah. But this also meant that he had to find a rational explanation for the crucifixion that people could accept so that they would decide to follow Jesus. His ministry provided an appropriate theological statement of who Jesus was, with the additional responsibility of explaining the death of the person he was telling everyone they should accept as Lord and Saviour!

It is doubtful, in Paul's mind, that Jesus or his teachings would be accepted if people continued to see the crucifixion of Jesus as Rome's response to a radical political figure. Paul knew about other radical anti-Rome Jewish prophet types who had tried to lead military rebellions against Rome (see Acts 5:36-37 & 21:38). Paul had to differentiate what had happened to Jesus to keep his experience separate from these other figures in Jewish history. He wanted to perpetuate the Jesus model as a teacher sent from God.

Put in that context, it is easier to be sympathetic to the issues Paul faced, and to understand how Paul chose to respond within the political climate of his day. The same Rome who crucified Jesus later killed Paul because he followed Jesus. It is not helpful to think of Paul as being out of step with Jesus. But it is important to note that Paul's explanation of the crucifixion (as helpful as that might be) is only one of several explanations offered by the Biblical writers. The early church was too busy sharing the good news of the message of Jesus to wrestle with theological ideas about how to interpret or explain why Jesus died on the cross. They just knew it had happened, it was horrible, but with the resurrection event on that weekend, it had changed their lives, and it could change yours also !

IV. The Resurrection Life

1. Introduction

Three days can be an eternity when one is in the midst of a gut-wrenching and faith destroying experience. For three years the disciples had seen what Jesus was doing and how he related to people who were suffering. They felt within themselves the hope that simply exuded from his presence with them. They did not just believe, they KNEW that Jesus was making a difference that could not be stopped. They could see it in people's faces, they heard it in his voice as he spoke. They knew life was going to be better, not just for themselves, but for everyone. In a strange way that they had never felt before, they began to believe again in a God who cared about them. They had a new sense of life-giving energy, and they were discovering that they cared about people, too. Somehow, the world was going to be different because of the presence of Jesus in it.

And then, it happened. Just thinking about it took the life out of their lungs, so that they found themselves just standing there, unable to walk and think at the same time. They could not imagine how they could go on. How could people do that? A week ago the crowd was shouting "HOSANNAH" and everyone felt they were on the edge of the most dramatic change that Jewish faith had ever seen. The Messiah, for whom they had been praying for centuries, was literally here with them, right now! Then just a few days later some of those same people were yelling "CRUCIFY HIM". Once again despair swept over them and they could do nothing but just stand there. They had to wake up from this nightmare and live this last week all over again. Maybe this time it will have a different ending.

The resurrection story is filled with accounts of despair being turned into hope, of death becoming life, of the past being swept away by the future. Without the resurrection, we would not be paying much attention to Jesus. At best, he might have been included as one of the teaching prophets in Israel, in the tradition of Isaiah or Hillel, but even that is doubtful. But then there was a resurrection that dramatically changed how the story was told because they discovered the ending had changed. It is doubtful, if not impossible, that Jesus would be celebrated as the promised Messiah if he had remained a dead body on the cross. The resurrection is God's response to the way of evil that had caused the death of Jesus. The world used death to solve problems, but in the resurrection we see that death is not God's way of offering redemption.

2. Resurrection in the Ministry of Jesus

The life-giving resurrection activity of God in Jesus is seen throughout the ministry of Jesus and is a central element in how the Jesus story is told. But not every life-giving event has to involve a death. The Jesus story is filled with living persons discovering new life – the Samaritan woman in John 4, the Canaanite woman in Mark 7, Zaccheus in Luke 19, the woman caught in adultery in John 8, the paralytic in John 5, the list goes on and on. To quote AMBS professor Dr. Howard Charles, "Jesus never attended a funeral that he didn't interrupt!" There is a fascinating trail of changed lives wherever Jesus went. Resurrection was not new for Jesus, and while we treat the resurrection of Jesus with special attention, there was a constant resurrection-to-new-life theology that was present in Jesus.

"I am come that they might have life" could be seen as the life motto for Jesus. But for many people the Christian message has become life-controlling in a way that throws a damper on the exciting realization of hope and new life. Many Christians have a tendency to tell other people that if they would just become like us God would love them too.

There are those who insist that Jesus knew all along that there would be a resurrection, so that all he had to do was endure the agony of dying before God would intervene and his life would be restored. This is not a persuasive reading of the text. The hints of pre-crucifixion statements by Jesus about his resurrection were written into the public ministry of Jesus after the gospel writers had experienced the resurrection of Jesus for themselves. The gospel accounts of the life and ministry of Jesus are not like the current daily evening news, where the press reports on statements made that day by important people. Jesus died in 30 CE, and the gospels were written about 35 to 60 years later. During these intervening years the faith community gathered for worship and told stories about what they remembered Jesus saying in a given setting. Their memory of pre-crucifixion events was innocently impacted by their knowledge of the resurrection event, thus they read their awareness of that event into the stories of Jesus that they were telling. Don't judge them for not being precise in how they told the stories, they were simply theologizing about historical events. This should be seen as a tribute to how deeply the resurrection shaped their memory of history. Even with our own experience, we still tell the stories of Jesus with a specific positive theological interpretation.

The early church talked about the resurrection as the activity of God in the Jesus story. They believed that the same resurrection power that raised Jesus from the dead was available in their own lives. But the new element was that one did not have to die to experience it. There are basic elements in the resurrection event that tell us that the human Jesus did not have advance knowledge of how this story would end.

That is important, because that is how most of us experience resurrection in our own lives. Resurrection is rarely planned for, or intentionally expected. Rather, our own resurrection experiences burst in upon us in the midst of suffering in our own lives. One does not plan to discover new life, it is within the involvement of God in human experience that we celebrate our own new life, and we give thanks whenever that happens.

For the disciples this was indeed life changing. After Jesus' death, the reality of his life took on more intense meaning as it shaped their lives. They spoke of Jesus in the present tense, not as a memory from the past. Even more important, the resurrection was God's vindication of all that Jesus had said and done. This gave the Jesus message new content and vitality for themselves.

The Biblical writers talk about the resurrection using simple statements, but none of them describe the precise event itself. No one from the faith community was present to see the actual resurrection activity. The story has two Roman soldiers standing watch, but they were not permitted to tell what they saw (Matt. 28:11-15)! This casts a creative methodology over the whole experience. Of all people to see the resurrection happen, only God would be so creative as to waste it on two unbelieving Roman soldiers! But perhaps that helps us see the creativity of God at work. How would the story be different if two devoted disciples (Peter & Mary?) had seen the actual event? How would that have shaped the story? (See the attachment from the Gospel of Peter, a 6th C. Apocryphal Gospel showing how the story expanded over the centuries).

So, when the Gospel writers report that "God raised Jesus from the dead" they are not describing how God did it, they are sharing their confidence that God was involved in that activity. They were not expecting a resurrection, but decades later as they were telling the story, they read back into the story words that imply Jesus hinted at it. So, writing after the event, they included statements to support their belief that this was really an act of God, and that Jesus knew that. Unfortunately, some of their statements from memory about the words of Jesus do not mesh smoothly with other statements made by Jesus during the events of that week.

3. The Resurrection Story for Paul

As did many other people, Paul experienced the risen Jesus in an unusual way. How that encounter took place is reported by Paul in narrative form in Acts 9,22,26. In none of the three accounts does Paul report seeing anyone, so we have no record of any physical or spiritual appearance. In Acts 9 there was a light and Paul heard a voice. Those who were travelling with him saw no one, but they also heard the voice. In Acts 22 & 26 Paul heard a voice and had a brief conversation with the speaker whom he identified as Jesus.

Not long before this event Paul had listened to Stephen present an intense retelling of Jewish history highlighting their constant stubborn rebellion against the leaders God had given them (Abraham, Joseph, Moses, the prophets, ending with their rejection of Jesus—Acts 7). It was a powerful presentation that had a profound impact on Paul. Did Stephen force Paul to think of Jesus in a new way? What if Stephen was right in how he told history? What if the followers of Jesus were right in how they talked about Jesus? Could Paul (who also knew his Jewish history) have been reflecting on Stephen's words when he heard the voice on that hot, sunny day on the way to Damascus. What if this new truth actually caught up with Paul in the words of Stephen?

The important focus for Paul was not the details of the resurrection event, but how his life was changed because of that encounter on the Road to Damascus. Paul captures this change with an important Christ statement in the form of a hymn of praise in Philippians 2. He introduces the hymn with the challenge *"let the same mind be in you that was in Christ Jesus"* (vs 5). He then writes of Jesus' life, death and resurrection. That profoundly simple account is a challenge to all followers of Jesus. Paul moved beyond describing the initial experience to describe a life that is lived. This new life put Paul on a direct collision course with Rome. To say "Jesus is Lord" (to have the mind of Christ) denied Rome's central claim that they were lord. The new life that Paul was living was a constant reminder of who was Lord in his life. Unfortunately the result for Paul was exactly what it had been for Jesus. Both men were executed by Rome because they chose to live the resurrection life in an empire that ruled by the way of death.

We should also note that Paul based his belief that God raised Jesus from the dead on his experience with the risen Lord on the road to Damascus and not on the empty tomb.

4. The Resurrection Body

"But someone will ask, How are the dead raised? With what kind of body do they come?" (I Cor.15:35). Scientists, Psychologists, Theologians and average everyday Christians have been asking that question for nearly 2,000 years. Unfortunately, these conversations tend to divide rather than provide uniting truths that guide us in being followers of the risen Lord.

Marcus Borg suggests that we should read the gospel accounts of the resurrection as teaching parables. He insists that seeing these accounts as parables in no way denies the public factuality of the resurrection. He urges us to move beyond just talking about the event itself to wrestling with the meaning of the event as told in scripture. Paul and the other New Testament writers talk about the event, but no member of the faith community actually saw the resurrection at the moment it happened. Borg suggests that the meaning of the event supersedes any discussion of the details about how it happened. In support of this statement he notes that both Paul and the gospel writers quickly moved beyond searching out the details to focus on the impact of this event on their lives. (Jesus, pp 261-292)

Paul speaks of the resurrection as an event in history. He says that Jesus was seen by many of his immediate followers and even by Paul himself (I Cor.15:5-8).Although in telling the story of his encounter with Jesus Paul omits any reference to seeing the resurrected body. When he talks about it he immediately shifts into using metaphors to describe the physical aspects of that experience. But he also says that arguing over the physical or spiritual aspects of that resurrected body is foolish (I Cor.15:36).

Living as we do in a very physical world, we easily assume that when we talk about reality we have to be thinking about a physical reality because that is the only reality that there is. Yet Paul is very aware of a non-physical reality, and he launches into a lengthy discussion that contrasts the physical body with a spiritual body.

For Paul, the resurrected body is similar to and linked with the previous physical human body, but it is not a return of that old physical body to new physical life. The previous physical body was the appropriate vehicle for delivering the message of God's New Way. Now that Jesus had been crucified, the message is reborn in a new, equally appropriate body. This is important for Paul. The message that is delivered by the body is of more importance than the body which is used to deliver the message. Thus the focus of the resurrection for Paul was the resurrection of the message, not the return of the original physical body. This new body was spiritual, yet the message being delivered was exactly the same as what had been delivered in the physical body.

We are left with the dilemma of how these two different bodies were connected. This new spiritual body did things the previous physical body could not do. It went through closed doors (Jn.20:26) yet the disciples could touch him (Jn20:27). Mary did not recognize him at the tomb (Jn.20:14) but the disciples recognized him standing on the shore preparing breakfast for them (Jn.21:1-14). Mary was told not to hold him (Jn.20:17, but Thomas was told to put his hand in the side of Jesus (Jn.20:27)

Paul explicitly contrasts this new spiritual resurrection body with the old earthly, physical body. *So it is with the resurrection of the dead. What is sown is perishable, what is raised is imperishable. If there is a physical body, there is also a spiritual body (I Cor. 15:42,44).* It is important to understand that Paul lived in a world that accepted the presence of spiritual beings with actual non-physical bodies. It is appropriate for Paul to say that the resurrection body of Jesus is not his prior physical body returning to life. Rather, it is a completely new and different body which is quite appropriate for the mission at hand. For Paul this resurrection body is not the old physical human body of Jesus that the disciples had lived with for three years.

Traditional Christian faith has used the resurrection to validate the divine nature of Jesus. But Paul's attempt to explain or clarify the physicality vs spirituality of this new body continues to raise questions. The central message of the resurrection does not focus on the renewed existence of Jesus in a physical body, but on the continuation of that God message that Jesus had been proclaiming for three years. In his discussion of comparative bodies, Paul is emphasizing that the body has changed, but the message has not. This new spiritual body is delivering exactly the same message that Jesus had been preaching in his physical body. The excitement of the disciples is found in their discovery that the crucifixion of Jesus killed the body, but did nothing to change the message. God's message of love is not dependent upon Jesus being present in a physical body. Paul's point is that the same message Jesus proclaimed in his physical body is now being proclaimed in this new spiritual presence. The body is different, but the message is the same.

The disciples discovered that the death of Jesus did not change the message of Jesus. The Spirit of Jesus was still with them as they remembered the things that Jesus had done, the message he had given them, and the promise that he would be with them always. Paul is convinced that this new spiritual body contained exactly the same message that Jesus had shared in his earthly ministry. Thus the heart and soul of Jesus was still alive. The new life Jesus had promised was still with them.

Paul insists that the message of Jesus, delivered via this new spiritual body had the power to change human lives, just as the physical presence of Jesus had changed lives. Thus, the heart of the Jesus message was still alive. The promise of Jesus to be with them was still very real because they experienced Jesus as being fully present with them as they remembered, shared, and lived the message that Jesus had given them when he had a fully physical body.

After the crucifixion, the disciples gathered together first in fear, then with amazing bravery as they discovered again and again that the message of Jesus was still life-giving. Everything Jesus had told them to do was still an accurate description of their task. Jesus had talked about loving enemies, about giving your life for others rather than killing others to save your own life. This is exactly what they saw being lived out in Jesus that terrible weekend when Rome crucified him. He was literally living the content of his teachings by dying rather than calling for those twelve legions of angels that were just over the hill. It was the living fulfillment of his message, and in that discovery, the message of Jesus took on new life for them. They found the heart and soul of Jesus and everything that he had done was still God's message of salvation. Rome could kill the messenger, but the message was still alive, being reborn in them with the task of sharing that message with others just as Jesus had done. And in that discovery the disciples found the excitement of new life. Their world had not come to an end, it was simply in transition.

Living as we do in a very physical, material world, it is easy to believe that any honest reality has to be physical. Yet Paul is very aware of the power of an idea to connect with the past and transform the present in a way that gives new life to the future. Paul believed that Jesus lives with and in us, as a powerful life changing presence that brings to life for us all that Jesus was in his life.

Thus, the new spiritual body of Jesus was able to deliver the message of Jesus just as effectively as the old physical body of Jesus had done. Only now, Jesus is present in ways that were not possible for Jesus with his physical body. Paul is fully persuaded that the loss of the physical body of Jesus did not mean the loss of the message. In this new spiritual body, Jesus lives among and within us as we share together, retelling the story of Jesus and allowing the teachings of Jesus to give birth to new life in new ways within us. The message of Jesus in this new spiritual body was exactly the message of Jesus they had received in the old physical body. Rome had not killed the message, and that gave them the courage to go on. The proof of this life changing message is seen in Pentecost, in Stephen before the Sanhedrin, in Paul on the Damascus Road, and in the lives of James, Peter, Andrew and the other disciples, who like Jesus lived the integrity of the God message in Jesus and were martyred by Rome for the same reason that Jesus was crucified.

During his earthly ministry, the focus of Jesus was on the God message of love and forgiveness, not on the nature of his physical body. When he called disciples he was making the point that the message needed to be shared with humanity long after he would be gone. The body of Jesus was simply the vehicle for delivery of the message. Now, for Paul, that old body was gone, but God had provided a new non-physical body that would be the vehicle for the delivery of the same message of God's love.

Paul uses one more metaphor for the new, spiritual body of Christ, and it is perhaps the most significant for Paul. Starting with the physical body of the man Jesus, moving to the spiritual body of the resurrected Jesus, Paul adds the church as the continuing custodian of the message (see Col. 1:18, Rom.12:5, I Cor. 10:16, 12:27, Eph. 4:12, et.al.) Paul sees each body as being an appropriate vehicle for the gospel message in its own setting. It was in the person of Jesus that the disciples first heard the message of God's New Way. When Jesus was crucified by Rome in an attempt to silence the message, a new spiritual presence kept the message alive for the disciples.

This new spiritual body affirmed that the Jesus message had not changed, and that God intended the message to live on for future generations. Now, Paul's 3rd body metaphor, the church, has the assignment of sharing the same message that was present in both the physical and the spiritual bodies of the first century. Christ is now experienced in this new body which has many members, yet one central message, namely the Jesus call for all people to live by the values of God's New Way. Thus all three body metaphors are linked together in the continuing incarnation of God's salvation message give us in Jesus.

The instructions given by Jesus to this 3rd body metaphor guide us in moving past the body itself to the original Jesus message about the presence of God's New Way for all humanity. Paul effectively keeps the focus on the future, recognizing that the body metaphor is not the message, but the vehicle that conveys the message for all nations. The task of this third body, the church, is the logical extension of the task given the disciples---to go into all the world inviting people everywhere to live godly lives wherever they are, knowing that the message of God's New Age never grows old.

Perhaps we should have the epistemological humility and ontological modesty to admit that the resurrected body of Jesus and the way the resurrection story is told does not fit easily into our human definitions of a body needing to have flesh and blood, bones and molecules (Borg, 289).

It should not be too much to acknowledge the cultural differences between the 1st and the 21st Centuries and the problems that arise as we try to bridge that gap. Especially when doing that destroys our focus on the central factor involved in the story---the Jesus message of God's love that lives on after his death and resurrection, rather than debating the physical or genetic nature of Jesus' body. The resurrection of the message seems to be the emphasis that Jesus put into his post-resurrection appearances with the disciples. They are told that the God message of transforming grace lives on   and that should continue to be the focus for their own ministry. Dwelling upon a factual reality within the story easily destroys the message intended as the gospel writers tell the story. This attempt to force an answer for the wrong question obliterates the life-changing power that is latent within the story itself. We are losing the Biblical message because our 20th century knowledge will not let us incarnate within ourselves the exciting story of new life that lies at the heart of the biblical resurrection accounts.

We are in danger of distorting the Biblical focus when we leave the message to argue over the nature of the body that delivers the message. It would be truly tragic if we were to lose the call of God to new life because we decide it is more important to stand around the empty tomb debating the physical/spiritual details of what happened. John Dominic Crossan still speaks truth: *"It is not that those ancient people told literal stories and we are now smart enough to take them symbolically, but that they told symbolic stories and we are now dumb enough to take them literally"*.
(Quoted at Radical Discipleship Seminar, Portland OR, 2008).

5. Resurrection in the Biblical Narrative

A focus on the resurrection as an inclusive event that offers blessing and salvation to all humanity because it is a God event, asserts that God's activity is not limited to a narrow slice of religious humanity. The Old Testament people of God drifted into an exclusive belief about how God liberated them from slavery in Egypt, thus proving (for them) that they had special, exclusive status as God's chosen people.

However, God used the prophet Amos to burst their bubble of exclusive privilege. Amos reports God saying: *"Are you not like the Ethiopians to me? Did I not bring Israel up from Egypt, and the Philistines from Caphtor and the Arameans from Kir?" (Amos 9:7).* The sting in this message comes when we note that the Philistines and the Arameans were enemy nations for Israel! Thus God's redemptive activity is intended for all humanity regardless of their particular religious or political identity. The resurrection declares that the basic God message still stands. *God is not willing that any should perish (*II Peter 3:9), should remain at the heart of the Christian Good News.

The resurrection confirms the Jesus message that God wills all people to live together in peace, to care for the poor, to heal the sick, and to care for the world we live in. Rather than saving us as an external act of God detached from us (that's crucifixion faith), resurrection faith confirms God's invitation for all humanity to be encompassed by God's love. This is Paul's counsel in Philippians 2:12-13 *"work out your own salvation with fear and trembling, for it is God who is at work in you, enabling you both to will and to work for His good pleasure."* Note that God is not at work for us, or even on us, but <u>in</u> us, helping us do the will of God in our everyday living.

This confirms the original inclusive message given to Abraham, the essential message of Torah, the core of what the prophets were telling Israel, and the central content of Jesus who sends all those who get the message into the world, spreading this God message of hope, and peace, and a better, more God-like world. See Matthew 28:19-20 *Go into all the world (*don't keep it for yourself), John 3:16 *for God so loved the world (*not just us), II Peter 3:9 *God is not willing that any should perish* (God is for everybody).

6. What Does the Resurrection Story Tell Us?

What does it mean that the stories told describing the resurrected body say that it still carried the marks of the death inflicted by Rome? This provides insight into the makeup of our own resurrected lives. New lives, yes, yet the presence of our own physicality remains with us. Newness in Christ does not mean perfection in our humanness. Stories of the resurrection body of Jesus did not deny the reality of the crucifixion, they simply adapted and overpowered that tragic event. Perhaps that is the key for us as well.

Resurrection does not deny our humanness. It teaches us to adapt and live our lives in this world as new persons in Christ. It does not shield us from human tragedy, pain and suffering, but it does show us how to respond in ways that do not inflict our pain on others via retaliation. We are to live with an awareness that even in our pain, God does not leave us to suffer alone.

The modern scientific mindset that dismisses the resurrection as a factual event also tends to dismiss the core element of the teachings of Jesus as being impractical in our contemporary world. This dismissive attitude enables them to turn their focus to the crucifixion because that is seen as an acceptable, historic event in which (in their minds) violence for redemption is validated.

Grimsrud suggests that in the telling of the crucifixion/resurrection story, the disciples found Jesus alive and life-giving in their own daily experience. It was not the crucifixion as a separate event that led them to proclaim God's salvation in the person of Jesus. It was the resurrection that clarified for them the message and identity of Jesus. That resurrection awareness gave them new life and they promised the same would happen for their hearers if they would only accept God's resurrection validation and join in being followers of this risen Lord experiencing the blessings of life in God's New Age. (Instead of Atonement: 204-206)

One of the first administrative tasks of the eleven was to replace Judas so that the number twelve would again be restored. The basic requirement for Matthias was not his presence at the crucifixion (none of the disciples were there— only the women and John were there). It was that he had seen the risen Lord. Thus it was resurrection, not the crucifixion, that was at the core of the new Jesus identity. But the disciples did not require that other post-resurrection audiences also had to see the resurrected Lord. Their own resurrection experience confirmed the person and message of Jesus, and that experience formed the basis for their invitation calling other people to see Jesus as the Messiah who was the teacher of God's New Way.

In this way, the resurrection stories expanded the experiential presence of Jesus for all humanity. As a human person, Jesus could only be in one place at a time. After the resurrection, as an expression of divine reality, they experienced God's presence with them in a way that was not limited to singular time or place. This brought an enormous expansion of all that Jesus was doing, for Jesus was now a living presence with his disciples in all places at all times. (see Matt 28:20 *I will be with you always,---everywhere---as long as time exists.)*

The resurrection experience also changes how we see Jesus as we live together with other world religious communities. Crucifixion faith focuses on how Christianity has something that no other religion has---a crucified messiah who died to save us from our sins, with an emphasis on how this is a blessing only for those of us who believe the right things. We tell other religious people that the blessing which we have will be theirs only if they become like us and believe the things that we believe about Jesus.

However the resurrection message has a more inclusive tone. It is an invitation for others to join with us in following the teachings of Jesus which create new life for all people. This is seen in the Matthew 25 story that urges us to team up with others in doing acts of kindness and love for all people. This Matthew account minimizes doctrinal beliefs about Jesus and focuses on being the presence of God doing the things of Jesus in daily situations. One does not have to cease being Jewish, or Buddhist, or Muslim to love your enemies, to feed the hungry, or to care for the poor. Familiarity with these religious writings shows us that such actions are also essential within their own religious systems. This raises the honest question, can one be a godly person within a religious system that is other than Christian? It also raises a more painful second question- -can one be a professing Christian and live in defiance of the teachings of Jesus about God's New Way?

Living the resurrection invites us to welcome others to join in resurrection living without first checking every detail of their organized doctrinal beliefs. People who are doing Jesus things (feeding the hungry, caring for the poor, being peacemakers, etc.) can join together and have more people be fed, or cared for, with the confidence that God will be pleased. And if confessing Christians are not feeding the hungry, caring for the poor, being peacemakers (doing Jesus things), perhaps our mission is to ask them why they are not doing these things, and invite them to change and join in following Jesus.

7. Resurrection For All Humanity?

The development of the disciples' message over those first decades gives credence to a question that is still raised today in some settings. Can a person who does not believe in the literal, bodily resurrection of Jesus live in the resurrection reality that is experienced in the teachings of Jesus?

Is it theological belief in the resurrection, or incarnational living in the life-changing content of the teachings of the resurrected Lord that leads to new life for people today? Do the resurrection stories save us, or do they validate the teachings of Jesus which guide us in experiencing salvation for ourselves and all humanity in God's New Way?

The conversation that Jesus had with Nicodemus that evening in Jerusalem gives us some assistance in finding an answer. Nicodemus asked Jesus to explain the meaning of being "born again" (Jn 3:4). At first Nicodemus picks on the literal imagery of going back into a mother's womb and starting life over again. Jesus picked up on that imagery and talked about the need for a completely fresh spiritual start that enables one to see God, God's will, our religious thinking, and our daily living in totally new ways. This is more than simply adjusting our belief patterns, or deciding on better ethical choices. He asked Nicodemus to change the way he thinks or deals with the assumptions that he has without thinking. From the instant that we are born, the world invests a lot of time and money teaching us how to think, and how to respond without thinking.

Jesus tells Nicodemus that people need to develop a whole new way of thinking. A new way that instinctively gravitates to God's way of being instead of the world's value system. We need to develop an awareness that God and the world usually do not think alike, and we need to be conscious of that. The world tells us that it is good to think religious thoughts as long as those thoughts don't violate the world's values about military might, about accumulating vast wealth, or about condemning the poor just for being poor. To be a Godly person means to be so infused with the ways of God that we see the difference between God's way and the cultural ways of the world. When we are born again, we begin to think as God thinks, and thus we respond to the ways of the nation without having to stop and debate within ourselves what we should do. That is what Jesus meant when he urged Nicodemus to be "born again".

How does this relate to resurrection faith? Jesus did not tell Nicodemus that someday the world will be saved BY GOD (as though our salvation will be an external event done by God for us). But Jesus said the world will be saved THROUGH him, implying that the world would experience God's salvation as it learned to think and live by God's New Way.

It seems that Jesus was expecting the Jewish people (and especially a gifted Jewish teacher like Nicodemus) to easily see the truth in what he was saying. He expected that they would experience a conversion from the traditional teachings of their day, and buy into the radically new, life changing teachings of Jesus, literally be born again, as they accept God's New Way for living.

8. Resurrection as Witness to Salvation

For Jesus, salvation is not achieved by, but is found in, living in God's New Way, and not as a detached, separate action by God without human participation. Was it God's original intention for Jesus to save the world, or was it to show the world how it might be saved? Throughout Biblical (Jewish) history, it is clear God gave the law, then the prophets, with the objective of helping the world experience God's intended salvation. Jesus came with a message that continued the original intention of both the law and the prophets. This is shown in what the resurrected Jesus said to Cleopas and his friend as they walked with Jesus on the road to Emmaus. *"Then beginning with Moses and all the prophets, he interpreted to them all the things about himself in all the scriptures."* (Luke 24:27) What a gift it would be to walk with Jesus and receive a lecture on Old Testament Christology!!

The resurrection as an event in history does not save us just because it happened, but the stories told about the resurrection do validate the person of

Jesus and the message he proclaimed in the name of JHWH, God of Israel, which is our salvation that also leads to the salvation of our neighbors.

The resurrection body of Jesus bore the marks of his death. And so for us as resurrection people we still live in the mundane commonness of our human existence, and our past will constantly be tugging at us to retreat back into our pre-resurrection existence. We need to remember that this old existence is where crucifixion still happens, where the way of death is still flexing its muscles. But we are resurrection people. Having the mind of Christ should be our comfort and also our challenge to be the contemporary body of Christ today. Because of Jesus, we know better.

This is where the promise that the God who raised Jesus from the dead is still in the business of resurrection, and will also raise us to newness of life in the midst of the living dead all around us (Rom. 8:11, II Cor. 4:14, 6:14). Jesus is no longer a flesh and blood figure, limited by being confined to the human dimensions of time and space. But in the new reality of human memory, he can enter locked rooms (prison cells, or our own religious prejudices); travel with people and not be recognized (be with the sick, the lonely, the outcast among us); vanish in a moment when recognized (leave without waiting for people to say thank you); be experienced in both Galilee and Jerusalem almost simultaneously (be present with wildly diverse people in far distant lands).

This is the message of the empty tomb. Jesus is not dead, he is no longer there, but among the living as a powerful presence that is still changing people's lives. The stories told about the resurrected Jesus gives authenticity to the instructions Jesus gave that we should care for others with the same intensity and compassion that he had when healing the sick, feeding the hungry, and befriending those who were all alone every day of their lives.

The most convincing proof that Jesus was raised from the dead is not found in debating theological issues from the past, but in the living, reconciling power of the body of Christ (the church) that is physically and spiritually present in the world today.

The challenge of the resurrection is not to figure out the technical, physiological answers for how it happened out there way back then. The most effective proof of the resurrection is when the living Christ comes alive in and with us. For if Christ lives in us, the lives of those who live around us will be given new hope for the day, food when they are hungry, a friend who visits them when they are sick, or a voice which speaks out for those who are imprisoned within locked cells or inside equally strong prejudicial beliefs and attitudes (Matt. 25:31-46,28:19-20).

When God raised Jesus from the dead (no matter how you choose to debate the technical questions regarding the nature of the resurrected body), the faith community saw it as a statement of God's intention that the resurrection message of God's healing presence is for all nations; for peace among people everywhere; of hope for a better tomorrow; of safety in your community; of being surrounded by people who care about you; of knowing what it means to be forgiven. It is a huge task, but the resurrection of Jesus was no small thing. The God who raised Jesus from the dead promises to be with us, as long as time exists, no matter where we go.

The primary issue for the church today in mission is not making sure we have the right theological answers for what happened to the physical body of Jesus on that Easter Sunday, but whether the risen Christ is experienced in us today so that the living Christ is still being presented *"alive by many convincing proofs". Acts 1:3.*

V. The Resurrection as Mission in God's New Age

The 14th Century St Teresa of Avila wrote a poem that the church continues to repeat

> ***"God has no hands but our hands to do his work each day;***
> ***God has no feet but our feet to lead others in his way;***
> ***God has no help but our help to guide them there today."***

It has been the accepted wisdom of the day that if the things of God are going to be done, we will need to be the ones doing them.

It is exciting to think about what it would mean if the church could accept the vision of Jesus for mission, and use that to organize our corporate and personal lives as we go throughout the world inviting people to live together in God's New Way as taught by Jesus.

This would mean a change in how we think about conversion. Jesus challenged Nicodemus to be born again in his thinking (John 3). Nicodemus was a devout Jewish rabbi who, by all standards, was not encumbered by any terrible sins that needed to be confessed. Jesus saw the issue as being that Nicodemus was caught up in the old way of thinking about God. Jesus did not call him to leave his Jewish faith to become Christian (there were no Christians yet when Jesus met with Nicodemus). It was a call to think in a radically new way about how one lives in response to Torah. If the church could accept this, we would still invite persons to be converted, but that conversion would not focus on telling others that they must leave their religious faith and join ours. Instead, it would be the Jesus call to leave the old ways of greed, death, war, lying, abuse (all things mentioned in the Torah and in the Sermon on the Mount), and commit ourselves to live a new life of peace, honesty, generous sharing, mutual respect, etc.

We could then join together with other religious people in doing the God things that Jesus had been doing. We would understand the teachings of Jesus to be incarnational rather than doctrinal, calling us to be peacemakers and healers, building relationships that lead to "salvation" (a better life for all persons). In our own complicated world, there are so many people who would benefit from the conversion message of Jesus in their own lives and in the lives of those around them. We could do this by focusing on how this is God's New Way for all people without insisting that they must first believe specific doctrinal facts that we have created within our own tradition.

Certainly God would be pleased to have people experience this new life in God's New Age without worrying about whether they attach the name "Jesus" to what they are doing. Jesus called people who were already religious to accept God's New Way of living, telling them that in living this New Way they would be fully included in God's love and grace regardless of their particular religious identity here on earth. In simple language, God's New Way always wins over sectarian religious identity.

The world would benefit, and those living in it would discover the joy of "salvation"---living in God's New Age where peace, human relationships, food for the poor, housing for the homeless, medical care for the sick and the elderly, would be a natural human reality.

Additional supporting comments come from the Book of Revelation. It is widely believed in some Christian understandings of faith that Jesus died on the cross to pay the price demanded by an angry God so that we sinful human beings might be saved and be assured of going to a new life in heaven when we die.

But John sees the holy city coming down from heaven to this earth (Rev. 21:2). His focus is not on how to get to this wonderful heavenly city, but how we prepare this world for when this heavenly city comes to earth. This reflects the Christian belief that we don't search for God somewhere off in the heavens, but that God becomes alive today in us just as God became alive for the disciples in the person of Jesus. John is telling us that now even the dwelling place of God is coming to us, rather than us having to get to it.

The point of John's vision is that the blessings of heaven should be the guide for how we experience life right here on earth. Things that were lacking in 1st Century Israel are present in free abundance in God's New Age. The leaves of the trees provide healing (health care for all?); there is no night there (people will not fear the darkness, but will live together in peace?); there is a river that has crystal clear water (an abundance of pure drinking water?); and joy will be shared by the residents of this wonderful place (all will recognize the blessings of this new life?).

In John's creative description, there is no mention of an exclusive entry into this sacred city. This changes our common message of faith. The Jesus message does not save us out of this world, but rather we are given the mission to heal the nations of this earth so that all people might walk in the light, sharing peace with all humanity, thus experiencing God's salvation in this life.

Such a vision would have dramatic impact on the life and mission of the church. We would gather for worship, not simply to celebrate how we have been blessed by God, but to learn how God would have us reach out in love to the community around us offering food, shelter, economic assistance, and healing for all those who share this geographic community with us. The Church will develop a community reputation that tells people "if you have trouble, if you need help, if life is hard for you, come to this community of faith, we will help as best we can".

We would have much for which we should give thanks and praise God. The spiritual health of a congregation will not be measured by a steadily increasing number of Sunday worshippers (although that might be the case), but by whether more people in the community surrounding the church know they are loved, that there is a place where they will be safe, where others will listen and care about what is happening to them.

We will continue to start new churches, not so much to save more people out of the world who will then join us in worship and support the church budget, but become local centers for mission where people will be invited to join with this new community of healing that is involved in loving, feeding, housing and caring for those who are being swallowed up or beaten down by the cultural, economic, and social forces that are so prevalent in our culture. The gospel that is preached in these mission outposts will invite persons to be "converted" from the worldly ways of death and abuse, and to join in life-giving ministries that are so badly needed all around us. Thus salvation would be experienced by us and shared with others at the same time.

Many churches are already discovering this mission. Here in Goshen, IN where I live, there is a congregation which houses a basic health care clinic, other congregations have food pantries, or offer jubilee sponsored funding for family emergencies. There is a cluster of congregations that have remodeled their buildings to provide private showers and private living space so that they might host homeless families on a shared, rotating basis. One congregations has refurbished a house where women are assured safety from abuse, or are given transitional help upon release from prison. Other churches provide English language instruction to improve family integration into the community, and Spanish language instruction so that we might do better at welcoming them. Several churches provide high quality day care for pre-school children of parents who are employed. Others have collected coats and boots in winter so that children will be warm. Churches met together in peace to stop construction of an ICE prison that would hold refugees who were being arrested for wanting to find new life in this country. It is truly exciting to see more and more congregations discovering again this call of Jesus to bring new life in God's New Way.

These local mission centers (churches?) will continue to tell the stories of Jesus, and use the Biblical texts for preaching, but they will also offer training in "righteousness" (conflict transformation, racial sensitivity, appropriate sexual interaction, economic counseling, etc). All of which will improve the human dimensions of life within the community. These churches will be known as safe places devoid of judgment or condemnation.

Community worship would involve celebration of new life and hope as people gather to give thanks for blessings experienced, and to renew relationships that remind us we are not alone and we certainly are not always perfect! Biblical stories would be shared as part of the tradition of storytelling in the faith community, but stories from other faith traditions would also be shared as appropriate for the population makeup of the surrounding community. The emphasis would be on what it means historically and currently to be members of this community of God's people who live among members of other faith communities.

I am not skilled, nor am I interested in knowing where to place blame for the ways we have misconstrued the message of Jesus so badly. I prefer to point us toward the future. There will always be those who will shout "heretic, liberal, ungodly" (or worse). It is helpful to remember that some of the Pharisees said these same things about Jesus. These attacks contain nothing new, yet they continue to be painful and discouraging. There will always be religious people who will continue to insist that only they have the truth.

Here again, a word from Jesus gives comfort and encouragement. Jesus warned of false prophets who come in sheep's clothing, but actually are ravenous wolves (Matt. 7:15-20), saying you will know them by what they do (by their fruits). But it is likely that we will always have conflict over defining who are the sheep and who are the wolves among us.

Here the affirmation and support of the broader faith community is critical. As members of God's New Way, we must be prepared to affirm, offer support, and stand with those who are criticized for daring to challenge traditional thinking (as Jesus did), or who are ostracized because they (as did Jesus) befriend persons who are different and not accepted in the faith community. How do we respond to those who dare to live in defiance of the prevailing forces of the dominant culture which still believes that war is the way to make peace, that exclusion is the way to build community, and that accumulation of still more possessions will lead to the good life?

In his own day, there were religious people who were critical of Jesus and his message. We should not expect that acceptance of the Jesus message about God's New Way will be any different today. Challenging the established patterns of religious thinking has always had its stressful responses. Long held beliefs are not easily changed, but the promise of Jesus to be with us as we live out this mission is still a living reality.

Those who have experienced community, who share this vision of God's New Way, know the blessing that comes from this participation. It is not something to be talked about in abstract ways, it is a life to be experienced. Jesus was the incarnation of God's love for all humanity. We are the recipients of that love. We will experience it best as we share this incarnation with others.

The good news of Jesus is that God's New Age has come to us right here in this life. We see in Jesus the living presence of God as an incarnation of what God always intended. It is found in God's dream for all humanity, yet it is experienced best as we participate with God in making it happen. It is realized as we share in the creative energies of God, being the incarnation in our own lives of God's love for all people.

We recognize that living God's New Way as Jesus did so deeply challenged the established religious traditions that the leaders attempted to silence him, and eventually they teamed with Rome to have him killed. We also recognize that still today, people who dare to be the living incarnation of this Godly truth are being silenced and some are even killed for their commitment to God's way of peace.

We reject the idea that God demanded that Jesus die so that others might be saved. We see the death of Jesus not as a unique act of divine intervention to appease the wrath of God, but as the tragic, yet understandable response of evil toward one person's commitment to live the righteousness of God in a sinful world.

We proclaim a contemporary message of hope for all people (not an ancient death that benefits only ourselves). We join hands to welcome others into the fellowship (not excluding those whose language, skin color, sexual identity, or cultural/religious experience is different from our own). We experience God in the diversity of creation (not trying to stifle diversity to protect our own identity). We share our blessings with those who are less fortunate (not hoarding for our own benefit at the expense of others). We walk together in commitment to be the incarnation of God's New Way that brings peace, justice, hope and salvation for all humanity.

This call for God's New Way dominates the scriptures. It is seen in the creation of Torah which was given as the guide for how the people of God would live together with their neighbors in their new land. The prophets pleaded with Israel to return again to a faithful reading and response to Torah, with the promise that this would bring healing to the land. Jesus referred to this theme as being at the heart of his message describing God's salvation in his hometown synagogue at Nazareth. The challenge is clear and simple: Are we willing to become the new people of God as followers of Jesus, giving incarnational expression to God's New Way in our own lives so that those living around us might experience God's love and salvation in their own lives?

May the grace of the Lord Jesus be with all the saints (Rev. 22:21).

VI. An Apocryphal Resurrection Narrative

There are numerous accounts of the resurrection included in Apocryphal writings. This one is from the Gospel of Peter 9:35 – 10:42
Greek Apocryphal Gospels: A New Translation, Lexam Press

9:35 Now on the night when the Lord's Day was drawing on, as the soldiers kept guard two by two in a watch, there was a great voice in heaven, 36 and they saw the heavens opened, and two men descend from there with much light and come close unto the tomb. 37 And the stone that had been cast at the door rolled away of itself and made way in part, and the tomb was opened, and both the young men entered in.

10:38 The soldiers, therefore, when they saw it, awakened the centurion and the elders (for they were also there keeping watch); 39 and as they told the things that they had seen, again they saw three men coming from the tomb, two of them supporting the other, and a cross following them.

40 And the head of the two reached to heaven, but that of him who was led by them overpassed the heavens. 41 And they heard a voice from the heavens, saying, "You have preached to the ones who are sleeping?" 42 And a response was heard from the cross, "Yes".

Bibliography

These books are not directly quoted in this study, but they have been influential in shaping my faith.

Ateek, Naim Stifan	*A Palestinian Theology of Liberation*	Orbis, 2017
Bailey, Kenneth	*Jesus Through Middle Eastern Eyes*	IVC Academic, 2008
Becker, Palmer	*Anabaptist Essentials*	Herald Press, 2017
Becker, Palmer	*What is an Anabaptist Christian*	Missio Dei, 2010
Borg, Marcus	*Jesus, A New Vision*	HarperSan Francisco 1987
Borg, Marcus	*Jesus: Uncovering the Life, Teachings and Relevance*	Harper 2006
Borg, Marcus	*The Heart of Christianity*	HarperCollins, 2003
Borg, Marcus & J D Crossan	*The Last Week*	HarperSanFrancisco 2006
Crossan, J.D. & N.T. Wright	*The Resurrection of Jesus*	Fortress Press 2006
Crossan, John Dominic	*God and Empire*	HarperCollins, 2007
Florer-Bixler, Melissa	*Fire By Night*	Herald Press 2019
Grimsrud, Ted	*Instead of Atonement*	Cascade, 2013
Grimsrud, Ted	*Theology as if Jesus Matters*	Herald Press, 2009
Kreider, Alan	*The Patient Ferment of the Early Church*	Baker 2016
Rohr, Richard	*The Universal Christ*	Convergent Books, 2019
Stassen, Glenn	*Just Peacemaking*	Westminster/John Knox 1972
Vreeland, Derek	*By The Way*	Herald Press, 2019
Weaver, J. Denny	*Nonviolent Atonement, 2nd ed*	Eerdmans, 2011
Weaver, J. Denny	*God Without Violence*	Cascade 2016
Wright, N.T.	*Simply Good News*	HarperOne, 2017

Printed by Libri Plureos GmbH in Hamburg, Germany